The Troubled Rhetoric and Communication of Climate Change

Despite an overwhelming scientific consensus, climate change remains one of the most controversial issues of our time. Focusing on the rhetoric that surrounds the issue of climate change, this groundbreaking book analyses why the debate continues to rage and examines how we should argue when winning the argument really matters.

Going beyond routine condemnations of the wildest statements made by religious fundamentalists or spokespeople for fossil fuel interests, the book explains the mutually exacerbating problems that permit many of us to greet catastrophic predictions with an equivocal shrug. It argues that the argumentative situation around climate change makes a certain kind of skepticism—"fair-minded skepticism"—not only possible but likely. The book also strikes a hopeful note, reminding us that people do change their minds in response to effective argumentation that appeals to deeply shared values.

Offering new insight into an ongoing academic discussion about the nature of argument and how it can be undertaken more effectively and ethically, as well as a new perspective on the rhetoric of science and technology, this book will be a valuable resource to students and scholars of climate change, environmental humanities, rhetoric, environmental communication, sociology, and science and technology studies.

Philip Eubanks is Professor of English at Northern Illinois University, USA.

T0383134

The Troubled Rhetoric and Communication of Climate Change

The Argumentative Situation

Philip Eubanks

Routledge
Taylor & Francis Group

LONDON AND NEW YORK

First published 2015
by Routledge
2 Park Square, Milton Park, Abingdon, Oxfordshire OX14 4RN

and by Routledge
711 Third Avenue, New York, NY 10017

First issued in paperback 2017

Routledge is an imprint of the Taylor & Francis Group, an informa business

British Library Cataloguing-in-Publication Data
A catalogue record for this book is available from the British Library

Library of Congress Cataloging-in-Publication Data
A catalog record for this title has been requested

ISBN 13: 978-1-138-06433-1 (pbk)
ISBN 13: 978-1-138-84118-5 (hbk)

Typeset in Goudy
by diacriTech, Chennai, India

Thanks, Greg.

Table of contents

Acknowledgements

Many of the people who helped me write this book did not realize they were doing it. Thanks to all those who chatted with me about climate change, book writing, and spending one's life in a productive way. Several people read drafts and offered valuable suggestions. For that, thanks are due to my wife Mary Lou, my brother David, my good friend Sean O'Leary, my colleague in rhetoric and writing Jennifer Maher, and my anonymous reviewers. I discussed many of the ideas in this book with my friend and mentor Greg Colomb, who passed away before the manuscript could fully take shape. I owe him my thanks on many scores. Thanks are also due to Northern Illinois University for awarding me a 2013 Summer Research and Artistry Grant. And, of course, many thanks to the editorial team at Routledge—Annabelle Harris, Margaret Farrely, Louisa Earls, and Bethany Wright.

Introduction

I grew up in the 1950s and 1960s when everyone was worried about nuclear annihilation. In my grade school, we crawled underneath our desks and covered our heads with our arms to prepare for the atomic apocalypse. As young as I was, I realized that this might not be enough to shield me from an H-bomb. Nonetheless, no one—neither kids nor adults—found the premise of the exercise absurd: that if the world was going to be destroyed, we knew what was going to destroy it.

It never occurred to us that the demise of human civilization might not come from any form of war but instead from an unintended consequence of prosperity. And here we are. Because of human activities that would seem to be far easier to manage than nuclear war, the world is engaged in an urgent debate about whether or not it has a future. A great majority of scientists have raised an alarm about rising temperatures and the all-but-certain devastation to follow. If the worst possibilities come to pass, books like this one won't matter very much for very long. The world as we know it just won't be here.

Nonetheless, the subject of this book is far from trivial. We cannot begin to grapple with the looming climate crisis unless we address the problem of public argumentation. As we face what may be the greatest existential crisis in human history, I want us to ask ourselves anew: How should we argue when nothing could matter more than winning the argument?

As a general proposition, I am not inclined to think of argumentation in terms of simply winning or losing. I share that disinclination with many other scholars of writing and rhetoric. We avoid talk of winning and losing for a good reason.

Most of us imagine a world filled with arguments waiting to be made, a world in which the best argumentation moves us little by little toward ever-elusive truths—a world in which argumentation is essential, but no particular argument needs to prevail. In fact, many of us think it would be a mistake to hope for any particular argument to win, or even try to win, because good arguments lead to even better arguments in a messy but ultimately constructive process. Taking part in this process is how we live ethically and meaningfully; it is how we make a better world.

That is not lofty idealism, either. Many times, it is both wiser and more realistic to think that argumentation—and persuasion of all kinds—ought to proceed according to Zeno's paradox: The best we can hope for is to move halfway toward an endpoint, then halfway again, and halfway again, never to arrive. That view requires us to respect others' ideas and to question our own judgments.

However, when it comes to climate change, the notion of endless debate seems to be not just dissatisfying but also dangerous. Some arguments must get settled. Some arguments need to be settled the correct way. Straightforward victory-seeking argumentation would seem to be the right tool for the job.

But that, of course, is the kind of argumentation that already dominates the public sphere, and it is—not just in my estimation—working very poorly. It has led not to victory or consensus but to stalemate and polarization. Indeed, what we are witnessing is a dismal case study in the failure of win-lose argumentation. The facts support one side and not the other. They have been established meticulously, expressed clearly, and disseminated widely. And yet the debate continues unabated.

I am aware of the potential oversimplifications that my just-the-facts framing of the problem might inspire. Over the past few decades, scholars of the rhetoric of science have worked hard, and convincingly, to show us that the scientific "fact" is not as stable and self-evident as people commonly believe (Bazerman; Ceccarelli; Fahnestock; Knorr-Cetina; Latour and Woolgar; Myers). Science, it turns out, is as rhetorically complicated as every other human endeavor—perhaps more so because it so successfully conceals its vagaries within apparently objective procedures and language.

Yet even if we adopt a clear-eyed view of the complicated ways that scientific knowledge is developed, we still have to recognize that, in the end, science deals with the physical world: that not all scientific judgments are equally valid. Among climate scientists, the idea that human activity is causing the Earth to warm dangerously is not the least bit controversial. The challenge is gaining broad acceptance of that fact among the general public.

On the way to acceptance, scientists' findings about climate change must pass through the crucible of public argumentation. And what a crucible it is. As Leah Ceccarelli points out, climate change is one of many issues coolly agreed upon by scientists but hotly disputed in public argumentation. She calls these disputes "manufactured controversies" ("Manufactured"). But manufactured or not, they shape public opinion, even among those who are not fundamentally against science or, as I will show in this book, not especially unreasonable. In other words, we face what I call a daunting *argumentative situation*.

In the chapters that follow, I describe what has gone wrong with our argumentative situation. I argue that the debate is plagued by a collection of mutually exacerbating problems that make the climate change debate more intractable than most of us already believe. Indeed, the debate is intractable in ways that render our usual responses largely ineffective.

The problems, in brief, are these:

- Although we usually see the climate change debate as a disagreement about science itself, both sides espouse nearly identical attitudes about science and objectivity, and neither recognizes the influence of its own predispositions on its attitude toward science.

- Although we often see opposition to climate change as a willful refusal to acknowledge facts, recent transformations in public attitudes toward facts and authority encourage us to confuse reasonable and unreasonable doubts. That confusion makes it difficult—not just for climate skeptics—to accept many public claims of fact.
- Although we usually see the climate change debate as a perversion of proper argumentation, it actually proceeds as argumentation typically does. Rather than arguing to correct error, all of us typically argue to preserve our intuitions. That allows basic human frailties, such as motivated reasoning and confirmation bias, to interfere with our judgments.
- Although we usually see the climate change debate as a competition between political and economic interests, the divide between pro and con—which is to say left and right—is much deeper. In the United States and in much of the West, we are self-sorted into opposing ideological camps. These camps adhere to deeply held moral foundations, which are evident in predominant conceptual metaphors and metonymies, including the key figures that shape people's attitudes toward the Earth itself.
- Changes in the way we communicate—driven partly by technology and driven partly by a new emphasis on visual communication—make attention rather than truth the commodity that is most desired. And in the course of vying for attention, all of the factors that tend to undermine rational deliberation are amplified.

Any one of these factors might by itself make the climate change debate difficult. But taken together, they create a situation that makes the worst of argumentation not only possible but likely.

The fact is, the current argumentative situation is not very encouraging. But it's not yet time to give up hope. In the end, I will offer some suggestions about how we ought to argue when "winning" matters. I do not insist that my suggestions are the only possible ones. However, I do insist that we need to think anew about what we expect from arguments about climate change and how we should undertake them.

Works cited

Bazerman, Charles. *Shaping Written Knowledge: The Genre and Activity of the Experimental Article in Science.* Madison, WI: U of Wisconsin, 1988. Print.
Ceccarelli, Leah. "Manufactured Scientific Controversy: Science, Rhetoric, and Public Debate." *Rhetoric & Public Affairs* 14.2 (2011): 195–228. Print.
—. *Shaping Science with Rhetoric: The Cases of Dobzhansky, Schrödinger, and Wilson.* Chicago: U of Chicago, 2001. Print.
Fahnestock, Jeanne. *Rhetorical Figures in Science.* New York: Oxford UP, 1999. Print.
Knorr-Cetina, Karin. *The Manufacture of Knowledge: An Essay on the Constructivist and Contextual Nature of Science.* Oxford: Pergamon Press, 1981. Print.
Latour, Bruno, and Steve Woolgar. *Laboratory Life: The Social Construction of Scientific Facts.* Beverly Hills: Sage, 1979. Print.
Myers, Greg. *Writing Biology: Texts in the Social Construction of Scientific Knowledge.* Madison, WI: U of Wisconsin P, 1990. Print.

1 What if we're wrong about what's wrong with argument?

The climate change debate is often quite sharp and quite basic. The "sides" cannot even agree on what kind of argument to have or whether to have one at all. Secretary of State John Kerry says unequivocally: "We should not allow a tiny minority of shoddy scientists and science and extreme ideologues to compete with scientific fact. … [W]e don't have time for a meeting anywhere of the Flat Earth Society." Contrast that with a remark from longtime conservative commentator and self-proclaimed denier, George Will: "When a politician on a subject implicating science … says 'the debate is over,' you may be sure of two things: The debate is raging, and he's losing it." Kerry and Will are hardly outliers. They express as well as anyone the hardened attitudes of the most important voices in the debate.

It is no coincidence, either, that both Kerry and Will take part in other polarized controversies. The argument that rages about global warming is not hermetically sealed. It is part of a larger public discourse in the United States and beyond. Nearly everyone agrees: Public argumentation is in crisis today. We're offended by its hostility, its unfairness, its frequent disregard of facts. And we worry about it. Unproductive argumentation hurts people in tangible ways.

Disheartening examples are easy to find. Just think of arguments about virtually any public disagreement—reproductive rights, same-sex marriage, gun safety, tax fairness. Yet even in this atmosphere of animosity and insult, the discourse surrounding climate change is especially confounding. What would seem to be a purely scientific question has become a focus of not just scientific disagreement but of every kind of disagreement.

On the web, the situation looks especially fraught. Consider this (not particularly egregious) thread from *City-Data.com*:[1]

Rikoshaprl
Obama, Reid and all the other fake filibustering, radical, left wing democrats state global warming is "settled science." They are full of hot air. Has any MSM [Mainstream Media] network aired the fact that 31,000 scientists have signed a petition stating they believe there is no man made global warming and that greenhouse gases are actually beneficial to the Earth? Over 9,000

of these scientists have PHD's. The Petition Project has been going on since 2009 yet it receives no attention from the global warming kooks.

Seabass Inna Bun
That's because it's garbage that came and went 16 years ago. Quote [from an earlier thread]: "What the 'petition' does in fact have is (approximately) 31,072 largely unverifiable signatures on slips of paper which um … isn't really exactly the same thing. Hmmm, a petition of scientists of questionable repute to challenge a mainstream scientific view using a failed argument from authority—there's a new one!"

......

The *Seattle Times* reported that it includes names such as: "Perry S. Mason" (the fictitious lawyer), "Michael J. Fox" (the actor), "Robert C. Byrd" (the Senator), "John C. Grisham" (the lawyer-author), not to mention a Spice Girl, a.k.a. Geraldine Halliwell: the petition listed "Dr. Geri Halliwell" and "Dr. Halliwell."

......

Notwithstanding its rather dubious methodology and fake names, that bastion of scientific rigor, Fox News, has quoted the petition in its news stories.

......

TrapperJohn
Burn 'em at the stake! In case anyone wonders, this project isn't funded by the Evil Koch Brothers, Big Oil, or any others. It's funded only by donations from the scientists who sign the petition, and the funding primarily is used for postage and similar.

......

SourD, responding to Seabass Inna Bun
You just can't wait for us to be taxed for CO_2 can you? Tell us, how does paying to produce CO_2 eliminate it?

......

Don Draper
The guy who started the petition was paid by Petroleum and tobacco companies. Money talks bs walks.

......

Seabass Inna Bun, responding to SourD
I couldn't care less about you or your taxes. I'm just proving right-wing denialists are liars. ("31,000 Scientists")

If John Kerry and George Will provide us with an example of highbrow polarization, the contributors to this thread show us the grassroots hostility that lurks not far beneath the surface of much public discourse about climate change.

It is fair to observe, of course, that even in this blunt web debate, all involved are ostensibly concerned with facts and their credibility. Rikoshaprl wants climate change believers to pay attention to a petition with 30,000 signatures of scientists. If genuine, that petition would seem to be worth more than a moment's notice. But Seabass Inna Bun doubts the petition's authenticity and supports his rebuttal by referring to the *Seattle Times*. He also injects some analysis of argumentative technique, citing "argument from authority."[2] Others plainly realize that the petition may be suspect because of its political provenance. That's why TrapperJohn preempts a likely accusation by saying that the petition was funded by the people who signed it and not by the Koch brothers. In turn, that claim is disputed by Don Draper.

It sounds almost like a genuine debate. However, the exchange of gotchas is beside the point. The *real* point seems to be mutual contempt. Rikoshaprl scorns "fake filibustering, radical, left wing democrats," who are "global warming kooks." Seabass Inna Bun sarcastically calls Fox News "that bastion of scientific rigor." SourD says derisively that Seabass Inna Bun "can't wait to be taxed." Don Draper calls denialist claims "bs." Seabass Inna Bun calls denialists "liars."

The exchange of comments is less a debate than an excuse to trade insults. It is not different in character and method from the climate change debate at large, or, indeed, from many contentious debates that characterize current public discourse.

A litany of complaints about the way we argue

My aim in this book is not chiefly to complain about the contentiousness of arguments about climate change. Indeed, what I hope to show is that the argumentative situation is affected by numerous factors that are both less noticeable and more damaging than its all-too-evident hostility suggests. But that hostility is, nonetheless, an important force in the argumentative situation. So it's only right to acknowledge what scholars, journalists, and politicians have come to lament with depressing regularity—it's real.

In fact, the sorry state of public argumentation has been evident for a long time. Let me comment briefly about three aspects of the problem that seem to gain the most notice.

1. Public arguments are about winning and little else.

Many observe that our politicians, activists, and partisan commentators would rather win than be right. Today, argumentative victory is not just an important goal; it eclipses all other goals. That win-at-all-costs argumentation is so dominant that it is hard to find other models. Something must be done.

Anxiety about all of this certainly shapes contemporary teaching of writing and rhetoric. Textbooks are honor-bound to disabuse students of the idea that "winning" is the only aim of argumentation. On the very first page of *The Structure of Argument*, Annette Rottenberg and Donna Haisty Winchell say, "Of course, not all arguments end in clear victories for one side or another. Nor should they" (3). In the opening pages of *They Say/I Say*, Graff and Birkenstein write, "Although argumentation is often associated with conflict and opposition, the type of conversational 'they say/I say' arguments that we focus on in this book can be just as useful when you agree as when you disagree" (8). Such cautions ring true. In fact, obviously true. Argumentation does not have to be a contest where my gain is your loss.

Yet the idea of noncompetitive or cooperative argumentation runs counter to deeply held cultural habits, which can be hard to accept. Consider this version of the standard warning. In *Everything's An Argument*, Lunsford, Ruszkiewicz, and Walters tell students that the Western concept of argument is usually "about disputation or combat," but "writers and speakers have as many purposes for arguing as for using language, including—in addition to winning—to inform, to explore, to make decisions, and even to meditate or pray" (5). I must admit that although I understand perfectly well what Lunsford *et al.* are saying, it takes some effort for me to make complete sense of it.

Perhaps I am not as good a person as I should be, but I ask myself these honest questions about why I argue: Do I really argue just in order to inform? Or is it to inform others about an idea that I favor? Do I really argue in order to explore? Or to explain the insights I've gained from my explorations? Do I really argue in order to make decisions? Or to recommend what I think is the best decision?

Then, I arrive at "to meditate or pray." If I think for a moment, I can imagine scenarios in which meditation or prayer do involve argumentation. I suppose that in those cases, I might argue with myself. But isn't meditation as much about *not* thinking as about thinking? Isn't prayer about praising, thanking, and asking? Where are the claims? Where are the reasons and evidence that support those claims?

To think of meditation or prayer as arguing requires a profound broadening of what counts as an argument. Lunsford *et al.* say that "everything" is an argument. However, it is one thing to recognize that a broader conception of argumentation may well be useful, and another for us to see it everywhere we look. Yet when we toss aside the Western default—arguing a point, arguing competitively—it can be difficult to say what is *not* an argument.

Some have pointed out how easy it is for textbooks and teachers to fall into old habits, despite the earnestness of their cautions. A. Abby Knoblauch writes:

> As we have seen, both *Writing Arguments* and *Everything's an Argument* initially define argument as more than attempts at winning or conversion, but the discussion questions, examples, and more detailed explications within both textbooks privilege an intent to persuade, illustrating for students the primacy of persuasion and either marginalizing or functionally erasing alternative processes or outcomes. (262)

Along the same lines, Chris Blankenship traces the patterned ways that textbooks warn first about the competitive impulse and then slip back into the frame of competitive or adversarial argumentation. This apparent inconsistency doesn't make a broader, more cooperative view of argumentation any less valuable. It simply demonstrates how deeply entrenched in our cultural habits the win-lose view of argumentation is.

One reason for its staying power is that well-established conceptual metaphors undergird our ideas about argumentation. These metaphors tell us, as Lakoff and Johnson point out, that arguing is *systematically* conflictual. In ordinary talk, we say that people *win, lose, overcome, strengthen, weaken,* and *defend* arguments. Even seemingly non-competitive metaphors can be tricky. We *build* arguments. But whatever is *built* can be *destroyed* by counterarguments. If our arguments *go in circles* or if our arguments *have holes in them,* we can *lose.* All of these expressions add up to a metaphor system that sets the parameters for thinking about argumentation. Call the main metaphor in the system Argument Is War, as George Lakoff and Mark Johnson do (3–4). Call it Argument Is Conflict. But whatever we call it, it is the frame that alternative ideas about arguing are up against.

The desire to set that frame aside comes partly, I think, from simple distaste. Especially in our current media environment, competitive arguing can be ugly. Yet there are other good reasons for rejecting the win-lose model of argument. Sharon Crowley makes this point well:

> Arguments can't be "won" in the way that basketball teams win. ... If I succeed in persuading you to change your mind about the injustice of preemptive war, for example, I have not "won" much of anything except your (perhaps temporary and lukewarm) adherence to this position. And by entering into argument with you, I put my own position at risk; during argument you may in fact convince me that in this or that particular case of preemptive war was just, in which case I must qualify my original claim. You can read this as a "win" if our relationship is competitive for some reason, and I suppose in this circumstance "victory" in an argument

> provides satisfaction similar to that achieved when, for example, the Phoenix Mercury finally wins a game. That is to say, just as we may extrapolate from "My team beats yours" to "My team is better than yours," we may extrapolate from "You accepted my claim" to "I am smarter than you." (33)

It is true, when we look closely at the world of argumentation, it is difficult to know who has won and who has lost. The more honest the participants, the less clear that division becomes.

2. Public arguments are presented as two-sided even when they do not need to be.

The metaphor Argument Is War is expressed in many ways, but all of those expressions conform to the same conceptual shape. It rests on a stable image-schema. If someone can *win* an argument, it follows that someone else has to *lose*. So the image-schema entails two contending sides, one combatant against another.

As complex as wars may actually be, with multiple aims and numerous combatants, we often reduce them to two sides—the Allies versus the Axis Powers, the terrorists against the civilized world. So it is with arguments. When we think of argument as war, the metaphor has a simplifying effect. Argument becomes a matter of claims and counterclaims, pro and con, convinced or not convinced, true or false. It becomes a matter of taking sides.

In political argumentation, this phenomenon is called polarization. Floyd Anderson and Andrew King's 1971 study of President Nixon's "silent majority" is often called a seminal statement on the rhetoric of polarization. They define polarization as a process by which "an extremely diversified public is coalesced into two or more highly contrasting, mutually exclusive groups sharing a high degree of internal solidarity" (244). Which is to say: polarization is not just about having opposing opinions. It is also, or mostly, about being different kinds of people.

Not surprisingly, the war metaphor appears in King and Anderson's description. Polarization does its work by creating a "we feeling" that requires "a perceived 'common foe' which the group must oppose if it is to preserve the fabric of [its] beliefs" (244). Nixon created the "silent majority" as a foil to the anti-Vietnam War demonstrators. It was an either/or proposition. Those who were not part of the "silent majority" were part of the "radical left." In Nixon's rhetoric, the "radical left" lumped together violent demonstrators with, for example, members of the U.S. Senate who opposed the war. Us versus them.

The issues have changed today, but it doesn't take much imagination to see how polarization continues to work in the same way. Yet if polarized argumentation in the past couple of decades is not so different in kind, it is different in breadth. Virtually all public argumentation is peopled by ever-warring groups. It has become almost impossible for us to imagine an argument that isn't composed of two irreconcilable sides.

No one explains the problem more cogently than Deborah Tannen in *The Argument Culture: Stopping America's War of Words*. She questions "the ubiquity, the knee-jerk nature, of approaching almost any issue, problem, or public person in an adversarial way" (8). In her role as a public intellectual, Tannen knows very well how public discussion constantly takes the form of war-like argumentation. She tells of the time she chatted amiably with a fellow guest before a radio appearance, only to be aggressively attacked by him on the air because, as he explained to her, such behavior is expected.

Her greatest lament is that such experiences are not limited to media appearances. She describes a panel at the Smithsonian Institution titled (without her prior knowledge) "The War of the Sexes." And when she participated in a discussion with an African-American playwright at a local theater, the flyer—to Tannen's and the playwright's chagrin—promised a conversation about the conflicts between Blacks and Jews (6–7).

Tannen doesn't claim that all conflict needs to be removed from argument at all times (few do), but she does worry about the consequences of this persistent emphasis on taking sides. When you take sides in an argument, she observes, argumentation can fail us: "Opposition does not lead to truth when an issue is not composed of two opposing sides but is a crystal of many sides. Often the truth is in the complex middle, not the oversimplified extremes" (11).

3. Two-sided, winner-take-all argumentation has poisoned the public square.

We cannot discuss argumentation without mentioning the discouraging state of U.S. politics and governance. It would be like discussing the Titanic and leaving out the iceberg. The truth is, it's difficult to tell whether argumentation has become hyper-contentious because of the political environment or the other way around. But most observers agree: To fix one, you have to fix the other.

That is certainly the view expressed by Al Gore (*Assault*), who believes, along with many others, that something has gone "terribly wrong" with our democracy (introduction). He bemoans a public discourse filled with "the rejection and distortion of science" (introduction), "the language and politics of fear that short-circuit debate and drive the public agenda without regard to the evidence, the facts, or the public interest" (ch. 1), and a world of communication in which "an incestuous coupling of power and money" has led to "the misuse of public power" (ch. 3).

The root of the problem, says Gore, is the way we receive information and the limited means citizens have for responding to it. Because of mass communication, especially television, citizens no longer participate in the "marketplace of ideas," which began in the Enlightenment and came into full flower in the world's great democracies, not least in the United States. And the main aim of the market-place of ideas has been abandoned—the obligation to seek agreement.

For Gore, writing in 2007, the Internet provides the best hope for restoring a genuinely "connected" populace. Since then, the Internet has become increasingly interactive. Blogging and social media have proliferated. Nevertheless, observers of public argumentation still despair. In the U.S., we seem to be mired in a public discourse that privileges image over substance, emphasizes controversy no matter how much common ground may actually exist, and adheres to a false "balancing" of viewpoints that allows mis- and disinformation to flourish.

Let me pause here to give the idea of "balance" special attention. It is especially pernicious. I feel its insidious pressure every time I write. I felt it, in particular, while composing the preceding three paragraphs about Al Gore.

I think that Al Gore sees rather clearly much of what is wrong with our public discourse. He is right that it is often filled with false and misleading information. I think he is right that democracy cannot function well without an informed, connected public—a "meritocracy of ideas" (ch. 3). Yet I feel uneasy citing him as an authority. I am painfully aware that Gore—former Vice President of the United States, two-time presidential candidate, and recipient of the Nobel Peace Prize—is a dicey authority to cite. In our polarized discursive landscape, he is as much reviled as revered.

And so I feel an urge to seek a balance—perhaps to cite a conservative voice who agrees with Gore. In our current argumentative situation, can anything be called "true" until the two warring sides both admit that it is correct? Short of that, I feel the urge to put forward equal and opposite complaints from a movement conservative about bias in the mainstream media. Should I do that despite my deep reservations about those accusations?

You see the dilemma. It is difficult to talk about our dispiriting argumentative situation without some temptation—in the name of fairness—to contribute to it.

Indeed, as the balancing game is played today, it won't be enough for me to cite, as I am about to do, a book called *It's Even Worse Than It Looks* co-authored by Thomas Mann, who hails from the "liberal" Brookings Institute, and Norm Ornstein, who hails from the "conservative" American Enterprise Institute. In their recent analysis of political extremism in U.S. discourse and governance, they dispute the notion that both "sides" are equally responsible for the problem.

They call it "asymmetric polarization" and place the blame squarely on the conservatives. "It is traditional," they write, "that those in the American media intent on showing their lack of bias frequently report to their viewers and readers that both sides are equally guilty of partisan misbehavior [but] the reality is very different" (51). They document the Republicans' sharp turn to the right and, in turn, blame them and their ultra-conservative allies for poisoning the public square.

Like Tannen, they point to the reflexive two-sides-to-everything model followed by the media. They write:

> The Fox business model is based on maintaining a loyal audience of conservatives ... MSNBC has adopted the Fox Model on the left, in milder form ... [and] CNN ... has settled on having regular showdowns pitting either a bedrock liberal against a bedrock conservative or a reliable spinner for Democrats against a Republican counterpart. (60)

That model, of course, reinforces the Argument Is War metaphor, and not only in the sense that all arguments must have two sides, but also in the sense that each side must be bent on the other's destruction. It's not enough for one of these sides to win. The other must lose.

Worse yet, it's not a fair fight. It is conceivable that a two-sides model could operate without so much vitriol. But the Republican Party, Mann and Ornstein say,

> has become an insurgent outlier—ideologically extreme, contemptuous of the social and economic regime; scornful of compromise; unpersuaded by conventional understanding of facts, evidence, and science; and dismissive of the legitimacy of its political opposition. (xiv)

That extremism contributes to a media environment in which "no lie is too extreme to be published, aired, and repeated, with little or no repercussion for its perpetrator" (61).

The problem extends, perhaps to Al Gore's chagrin, into cyberspace. Mann and Ornstein write of false political anecdotes that "in their modern, Internet-driven form ... share an unexpected trait: Most of the time, Democrats (or liberals) are the ones under attack" (66). Although some Internet mischief has been aimed at conservatives, "when it comes to generating and sustaining specious and shocking stories, there's no contest" (66). The award goes to conservatives and Republicans.

Mann and Ornstein make a good case. Yet I am uneasy about taking that harsh condemnation as my starting point—even if the evidence for it is strong, even if it aligns with my own observations. I can't help it. I ask myself: Isn't there some way for me to be fair and balanced?

A prayer is not an argument

If observers are right about the state of public argumentation, there seems to be very little we can do about it—short of somehow returning, as Al Gore suggests, to a meritocratic marketplace of ideas in which sound arguments prevail in the end. Which is to say: We need to become better people and, even more daunting, to convince our opponents to become better people too.

At this historical moment, that kind of solution seems to me inadequate or, at least, out of reach. The argumentative situation appears to be intractable. We do suffer from an argue-to-win cultural model, we do divide most public arguments into two combating sides, the public square is poisoned, and one side does offend more than the other.

One way to address the problem might be to abandon argumentation altogether, as one delegate did at the 2012 United Nations Conference on Climate Change in Doha, Qatar. The delegate was Naderev Sano from the Philippines. He had evidently lost all faith in the power of reason alone. In the aftermath of a devastating storm in his country, which was double the size of the one that devastated the East Coast of the United States in 2012, he delivered a desperate plea.

I heard it on the radio and was riveted by Sano's inability to contain his emotion. He begins with a dignity that befits the occasion:

> An important backdrop for my delegation is the profound impacts of climate change that we are already confronting. And as we see here, every single hour, even as we vacillate and procrastinate here, we are suffering. Madam Chair, we have never had a typhoon like Bopha, which has wreaked havoc in a part of the country that has never seen a storm like this in half a century.

Soon, his dignified tone begins to crumble. You begin to hear his voice waver:

> Finally, Madam Chair, I'm making an urgent appeal, not as a negotiator, not as a leader of my delegation, but as a Filipino. I appeal to the whole world. I appeal to the leaders from all over the world to open our eyes …

As he finishes his plea, he struggles to maintain his composure, but you can hear that he is crying:

> … to the stark reality that we face. I appeal to ministers.
> The outcome of our work is not about what our political masters want. It is about what is demanded of us by seven billion people. I appeal to all— please, no more delays. No more excuses. Please, let Doha be remembered as the place where we found the political will to turn things around. ("This Week")

Some might see this as an argument of sorts. However, it is not an argument that invites discussion—not the kind that asks its audience to weigh evidence or to reason carefully. Sano's message is not "consider my claim and act accordingly"; it is "please help us."

Desperate pleas have a time and place. We often turn to prayers and supplications when rational argument has failed. I am entirely sympathetic to Mr. Sano. However, I do not think it is time to give up on argument. In fact, I fear that those who are deaf to persuasive arguments are equally deaf to emotional pleas.

Notes

1 I've edited for brevity but not for standard punctuation and spelling.
2 I realize that Seabass Inna Bun could be female. In fact, I can't be certain of the gender of any of the contributors to this exchange.

Works cited

"31,000 Scientists Believe There Is No Man Made Global Warming." Thread. City-data. com. March 14, 2014. Web. 15 March 2014.

Blankenship, Chris. *Metaphors of Argumentation in First-Year Writing Classes*. Northern Illinois University, 2012. Ann Arbor, MI: U of Michigan, 2012. Print.

Crowley, Sharon. *Toward a Civil Discourse: Rhetoric and Fundamentalism*. Pittsburgh, PA: U of Pittsburgh, 2006. Print.

Gore, Albert. *The Assault on Reason*. New York: Penguin, 2007. iBook file.

Graff, Gerald, and Cathy Birkenstein. *They Say/I Say: The Moves That Matter in Academic Writing*. New York: W.W. Norton, 2010. Print.

King, Andrew A., and Floyd Douglas Anderson. "Nixon, Agnew, and the 'Silent Majority': A Case Study in the Rhetoric of Polarization." *Western Speech* 35.4 (1971): 243–55. Print.

Kerry, John. "Remarks on Climate Change," Department of State. 16 Feb. 2014. Web. 11 Aug. 2014.

Knoblauch, A. Abby. "A Textbook Argument: Definitions of Argument in Leading Composition Textbooks." *College Composition and Communication* 63.2 (2011): 244–68. Print.

Lakoff, George, and Mark Johnson. *Metaphors We Live by*. Chicago: University of Chicago Press, 2003. Print.

Lunsford, Andrea A., John J. Ruszkiewicz, and Keith Walters. *Everything's an Argument: With Readings*. Boston: Bedford/St. Martin's, 2007. Print.

Mann, Thomas E., and Norman J. Ornstein. *It's Even Worse than It Looks: How the American Constitutional System Collided with the New Politics of Extremism*. New York: Basic, 2012. Kindle file.

Rottenberg, Annette T and Donna Haisty Winchell. *The Structure of Argument, Eighth Edition*. Boston: Bedford/St. Martin's, 2011.

Tannen, Deborah. *The Argument Culture: Stopping America's War of Words*. New York: Ballantine, 1999. Print.

"This Week." *This American Life*. NPR. 7 December 2011. Radio.

Will, George. *Fox News Sunday*. February 15, 2014. Television.

2   The trouble with audience

I began this discussion by asking how we should argue when we really must "win" an argument. To consider that question well, it won't do for us to finesse the meaning of win or to be fanciful about what genuine argumentative victory looks like.

We could say that when an argument goes well, everyone "wins." Knowledge is advanced, and so we all benefit. That's an intriguing way to think about winning—all victory and no defeat. However, it's credible only in the way the phrase "win-win situation" is credible. "Win-win" entered the lexicon because it was a *new and improved* version of winning, one that preserved the warm feeling of victory and banished the unpleasant fact that winning and losing are usually a matched set. In a must-win argumentative situation, such as we face with climate change, it won't be enough for sound arguments to win; specious arguments must lose.

Yet it doesn't help us much to rely on adversarial frameworks such as Argument Is War and Argument Is A Game. Consider again Sharon Crowley's disanalogy: Winning an argument is *not* like winning a basketball game. Arguing is different from basketball, Crowley says, because "If I succeed in persuading you to change your mind ... , I have not 'won' much of anything ... " (33). In other words, unlike basketball, argument is not a zero-sum game in which my win is necessarily your loss. True enough.

There is another reason why the war (or sports) metaphor doesn't solve the argumentative problem. For some adversarial arguments, one side genuinely has something to win, and the other side has something to lose. However, the "sides" almost never aim to get an opponent to accept a claim, and victory rarely comes when the "losing side" capitulates. Changing the minds of steadfast opponents certainly cannot be the way to win the climate change debate. Is there any chance—even a tiny one—that climate scientists will abandon their findings and join the climate change deniers? Will climate change deniers see the light and agree with mainstream climate scientists? In rare cases, such things do happen. But it's difficult to imagine them happening often enough to make a difference in what we do about the warming planet.

Winning the climate change argument is not a matter of convincing an opponent. It's a matter of swaying the public at large in order to win a political fight.

Politicians who win an election may have won an argument, in a sense. But they haven't won it by getting their opponents to change their minds. They have prevailed by getting a majority of observers—voters—to side with them. When that happens, both the politicians and their adherents win. The other side may lose the vote, but they seldom concede the argument. Indeed, they usually vow to go on arguing.

So let me amend my opening question. How should we argue when we really must win the argument and *when victory is a matter of convincing not an opponent but a diverse assemblage of observers?* Climate scientist Michael Mann thinks in exactly those terms. In his book on the "climate wars," he repeats an aphorism often attributed to Mark Twain: "Never argue with a fool. Onlookers may not be able to tell the difference" (ch. 8). The problem is, as Mann has learned, avoiding the argument is not an option. Convincing onlookers is difficult because, in point of fact, they cannot always distinguish a sound argument from a lie.

The case of Erin

In 2011, the public radio program *This American Life* broadcast a story called "Climate Changes, People Don't," which sheds a helpful, if somewhat discouraging, light on what it can mean to argue for the sake of a third party ("Kid Politics"). Much of what strikes me about the broadcast is the way people's words are verbally accented to express conviction, reservations, and more. *This American Life* is available on the web for free streaming, so I encourage you to compare your impressions (and prejudices) with mine.

First impressions

Host Ira Glass opens the story by describing a 14-year-old young woman he met at a Glenn Beck rally in Washington, D.C. We hear him as he first engages the young woman, Erin, in conversation at the rally. She's well-spoken and polite. I daresay that she is the kind of young person most parents and teachers dream about. But, of course, there is a rub. As we might guess, she is an ardent fan of the extreme right-wing commentator Glenn Beck. She watches his television show every day. She says that she knows it's an "opinion show." So, for her, it's merely a "jumping off point" so that she can do her "own research."

From the beginning, then, we have good reason to doubt that Erin is an objective evaluator of public issues. Even though her impeccable diction gives the impression of high intelligence, she is very young and, perhaps, not fully equipped to judge Glenn Beck's credibility. Furthermore, her claim that she does additional research is not particularly reassuring. After all, if the jumping off place for her research is Beck's fevered and sometimes tearful diatribes, the direction of her research is likely to be a bit skewed.

Erin is also undermined by a situation that she cannot overcome, no matter what her age or what commentator she idolizes. Americans in the early twenty-first century all know from sad observation that our politics and public argumentation are not to be fully trusted. Erin may claim to be an objective observer, a non-combatant whose aim is merely to ascertain the facts. But genuine non-combatants (recently dubbed *low-information voters*) are a distinct minority in the United States today. As Mann and Ornstein explain:

> The style and tone of partisan debate is often unsettling to ordinary citizens. But … critical segments of the general public have been pulled in the same directions as political elites. Voters are more polarized than nonvoters. More educated, informed, and engaged voters are more polarized than less educated, informed, and engaged voters. (46)

Against that backdrop, many of the things we might take to be hopeful signs, such as intelligence and a commitment to being well informed, should probably give us pause.

Indeed, the faintest whiff of politics is a red flag when it comes to expecting a fair hearing. Erin provides us with a very large red flag when Ira Glass asks her about global warming. Even though she has just acknowledged that Beck's show is opinion-based and assured us that she does her own research on public issues, it's difficult to expect her to follow mainstream thought when she says: "Global warming is propaganda. That's what I believe." She is a committed global warming denier.

That impression is reinforced when she confirms with a knowing laugh that, yes, global warming is taught in school. She keeps her disagreements respectful, she tells Glass. But her strategy is to answer test questions according to what the book says, not to be convinced by what teachers tell her is right. For her, respect doesn't mean granting teachers and scientists authority over their subject. It means listening quietly while remaining unconvinced.

If you are a climate change scientist or just someone who is deeply concerned about global warming, Erin does not provide much reason for hope. To be honest, I immediately pegged her as a committed partisan hopelessly caught up in anti-science propaganda. Yet when Ira Glass speaks with her at greater length, things turn out to be more complicated. Erin may be a committed partisan, but she may also be a fair-minded observer who, reasoning to the best of her ability, reaches (what I think is) the wrong conclusion.

What do we want from Erin anyway?

For the moment, I would like to put off worrying about how we might overcome people's biases or, if you prefer, their cultural and ideological positions. I would rather ask: If Erin is the arbiter of the climate change debate, what do we want from her? And could she possibly provide us with that?

That question is somewhat different from what has been considered extensively in rhetoric and composition studies. Scholars are more concerned with multiple audiences, discourse communities, genre knowledge, and geographical and ideological locations. Indeed, the scholarly literature on writing and audience is vast, and it complicates what we can mean by audience. To mention just a few influential statements on the subject, Lisa Ede and Andrea Lunsford have discussed audiences that are addressed (actual audiences that can be specified) and audiences that are invoked (audiences that are cast in roles that writers ask them to play). J.P. Mathes and Dwight Stevenson have described the interplay of multiple audiences—immediate, primary, and secondary. Scholars such as James Porter and Anne Blakeslee have focused on writers' and audiences' shared membership in a discourse community. And Peter Elbow has touted the virtues of ignoring audiences altogether ("Closing My Eyes").

It should come as no surprise to us, then, that an arguer's relationship with Erin, or anyone, is likely to be complex and difficult to manage. All audiences are composed of people who come from somewhere and who bring to every argumentative situation their ideologies and habits of mind. No credible scholar of writing and rhetoric relies solely on the now antiquated "reasonable person," an avatar of pure intelligence and unfailing fairness. Let's accept that point.

But let's also recognize that when it comes to argumentation, we are ever hopeful. We have expectations of readers (and listeners) that make us believe that our efforts are worth the trouble. Once again, composition textbooks can tell us something about our most resilient ideas.

In *Everything's an Argument*, Andrea Lunsford *et al.* present an admirably thick description of audience that covers, in keeping with all of the scholarship that has come before, every imaginable possibility. Their inventory includes "the person sitting across from you when you negotiate a student loan, the 'friends' who join you in a social network, and the ideal readers that you imagine for a paper or editorial you write" (5).

Of course, this "ideal reader" requires some imagination. Thus, say Lunsford *et al.*, writers conjure up "intended readers." They explain to their own intended readers, "You are our intended reader, and ideally you know something and might even care about the subject of this book. Though we don't know you [the reader] personally, we see you in our mind" (28). Similarly, the writer can have an invoked audience, a kind of reader who is named and is expected to read through a certain lens. A step beyond that, Lunsford *et al.* discuss "real" readers, "who may not be among those the writer originally imagined or called forth" (30).

That's a lot of possible readers to consider. Yet Lunsford *et al.* have familiar expectations of audiences—expectations that I suspect most of us share. Because the argument about climate change is, at root, about scientific fact, I'll focus on what they expect from audiences for factual claims.

Lunsford *et al.* use the example of the ivory-billed woodpecker. Not long ago, *Science* published a paper that presented evidence for seven or more sightings of the presumed-extinct bird. Those sightings did not convince all ornithologists. Some ornithologists, though, were more receptive after hearing audio of purported ivory-billed woodpecker calls, and even more ornithologists were convinced by analyses of the flight pattern of the mystery bird in a fuzzy video recording. Lunsford *et al.* sum up the problem this way: As for all arguments of fact, the challenge is "to find sufficient *evidence* for a claim to satisfy a *reasonably skeptical audience* (in this case, of scientists, naturalists, and birders)" (209–11, emphasis added).

In other words, we have a right to expect a few things from an audience when there is a factual dispute. First, we can expect them to be open-minded, though not a pushover. Second, we can expect their objections to be reasonable. Third, buried a little deeper, we expect them to agree on the terms of the argument. Arguments of fact should rise or fall based on the evidence. We expect audiences to voice disagreements about the evidence—whether it is enough, whether it is the right kind, whether it is trustworthy. But disagreements about whether evidence matters—that we can't abide.

We all know, of course, that our expectations are not always met. For controversial topics, such as climate change, ordinary realism tells us that zealots will have a difficult time being open-minded and agreeing on the terms of an argument. Still, common sense tells us that a third-party—a non-combatant, for whom a change of mind or heart incurs little risk—ought to able to behave as a reasonably skeptical, fair-minded arbiter. And that is where Erin muddies the waters.

Erin and the evidence

For better or for worse, I have already expressed my pessimism about Erin. Maybe my reflexive skepticism is part of the problem with the current argumentative situation. Surely I am influenced by others who lean more to the left than to the right and who are impatient with what seems to be an anti-science bias.

But Ira Glass undertook a small experiment with Erin that both confirms and confounds my skepticism. He invited Erin into the studio and put her remotely in touch with climate scientist Roberta Johnson, who is the Executive Director of the National Earth Science Teachers Association. She studies the climate at the National Center for Atmospheric Research and develops curricula for teaching young people about climate science. Glass asked her to talk to Erin about the best evidence available for climate change. Erin's role was just to say whether or not she was convinced.

The conversation between Dr. Johnson and Erin is strikingly different from the "conversations" we've grown accustomed to in so many venues. It is polite, respectful, and informative. After some cordial if somewhat stiff greetings, Dr. Johnson presents Erin with evidence for manmade, often called anthropogenic, climate change. It is a distillation of the scientific findings that have convinced mainstream scientists worldwide that the Earth is warming to the point of catastrophe because of human activity.

Dr. Johnson says that extensive measurements show that temperatures across the Earth are, in fact, increasing significantly, that permafrost is thawing, and that sea level is rising. This increase in temperatures, she explains, coincides with rising levels of carbon dioxide and other greenhouse gases in the atmosphere. She describes a particularly compelling kind of evidence—scientific analyses of ice cores, long tubes of ice extracted from Antarctica and Greenland and studied in scientists' labs.

These cores give scientists a chronological record of the composition of the atmosphere (including dust, volcanic debris, and carbon dioxide). Thus they have a precise way of tracking temperatures and CO_2 over the course of 420,000 years. The correlation is unmistakable between increases in temperatures and increases in CO_2. Given the Earth's position in relation to the sun, we have far too much CO_2. What's more, scientists have analyzed the type of CO_2 that is currently in the atmosphere, and it is "lighter in its isotopic ratio than it should be if it was from a natural source." It is CO_2 produced by fossil fuels.

If the audience meets our expectations, all of that would seem plenty enough to settle the question. Evidence has been provided. It is good evidence. In fact, as prosecutors often say, it is a mountain of evidence that points in only one direction. It's argument over. Unless, of course, the audience fails to agree on the rules of the argumentative game either by refusing to fairly evaluate the evidence or by refusing to grant the importance of evidence at all.

That is, of course, what I feared: that perhaps Erin would have a King James Bible secreted in her backpack, and that she would suddenly point to the verse in which God promises never again to flood the earth (*Genesis* 9:11). Not long before this broadcast, John Shimkus, a Republican representative from Illinois and chair of the House of Representatives Energy Subcommittee on Environment and Economy, had done just that (Samuelsohn). And Glenn Beck's radio comrade-in-arms, Rush Limbaugh, insists that one must be an atheist or agnostic to believe that humans could destroy what only God could create (Taylor-Miesle). But Erin takes a different tack.

She is equivocal. She cites counterevidence that she has discovered in her—as she once put it to Ira Glass—"own research." She says that she is not particularly convinced:

> I feel like there are still holes in the theory. Like the arguments that the highest temperatures that they've discovered have been in the 12th century. And that the satellite images that have been taken, that have shown the shrinking of the ice caps, were not entirely correct. And that they've taken other pictures that show that there isn't nearly as much melting as they thought.

As Glass explains in his narration, she also mentions "Climategate," the international kerfuffle based on an exposé of scientists' e-mail messages.

It's no surprise that Erin has found claims that contradict what Dr. Johnson has told her. Erin may have perused the popular denialist websites *ClimateDepot.com* or *WattsUpWithThat.com* or any of the dozens of books and websites that counter mainstream climate science with, to put it mildly, vigor. Whatever her sources, they very likely blend factual disputation with attacks on climate scientists' characters and competencies. One typical denialist book, *Global Warming False Alarm*, is authored by Ralph Alexander, who is "a senior marketing analyst in environmentally friendly materials at a small Midwest consulting firm" with "a Ph.D. in physics from Oxford University." Here is a sampling of his line of attack:

> If climatologists' conclusions and prognostications for the future were based on solid experimental science—the hallmark of genuine science—there would be good reason to believe them. But ... the whole architecture of man-made global warming depends on unbridled faith in deficient computer models. And the poor science is compounded by the all-too-human need of climate scientists to preserve their jobs and research funding by reinforcing the prevailing wisdom on global warming.
>
> ...
>
> It's definitely possible in principle that adding to the store of existing greenhouse gases by putting more CO_2 into the atmosphere could increase temperatures. ... But the total amount of CO_2 in the Earth's atmosphere is still only very small: about 390 parts per million, or less than one twentieth of a percent. It takes an awful lot of CO_2 to make an appreciable difference.
>
> ...
>
> The term urban heat island refers to the warming generated by people living in cities, which are always significantly warmer than surrounding areas because concrete, asphalt and buildings tend to soak up heat. Heat islands introduce bias into temperatures that are averaged over both city and rural land areas, causing average temperatures to be overstated. ... The IPCC [Intergovernmental Panel on Climate Change], however, in its ongoing quest to make all its data conform to the CO_2 global warming hypothesis essentially ignores this data contamination.
>
> ...
>
> The distinctly noticeable warm spell seen around the year 1000 is known to historians as the Medieval Warm Period. ... The cool period centered around the year 1650 has been labeled the Little Ice Age. ... Yet the Third Assessment Report [of the IPCC] in 2001 told a radically different story. All of a sudden the Medieval Warm Period and the Little Ice Age had disappeared! In their place was a fairly flat-looking graph with few temperature ups and downs until the beginning of the present climb around 1900—a chart that now bore a remarkable resemblance to the modern CO_2 record, looking like the shaft and blade of a hockey stick on its side. (ch. 2)

These points are countered convincingly by mainstream climatologists. They follow genuine scientific procedures; they demonstrate that 390 parts per million of CO_2 in the atmosphere is not small but dangerously large (hence the activist Bill McKibben's website *350.org*, which campaigns to reduce levels to 350 parts per million); they have taken urban heat islands into account in their calculations; and they are well aware of the Medieval Warming Period and the Little Ice Age, both of which figure into the IPCC's so-called "hockey stick" graph.

Likewise, Roberta Johnson responds to each of the objections raised by Erin. But Erin remains unconvinced—which is not the same as "in denial." She's listened to Dr. Johnson. But she's read material from other sources that she finds equally credible. And so she has checked *undecided*. That may seem to contradict her earlier statement that global warming is a hoax. But it may not. The case for climate change, like a case for the prosecution, must be made to a high level of certainty or it is not made at all. What Erin may be rejecting is the level of certainty attached to scientists' claims. If global warming is no more than a *maybe*, then their claims are false or as hyperbolically put, a hoax.

If that is her concern, she is in good company. One well-known climate scientist, the chair of the School of Earth and Atmospheric Sciences at the Georgia Institute of Technology, has ruffled many of her colleagues' feathers by rejecting the level of urgency and certainty of climate scientists' statements. Judith Curry states the following:

> I don't know how concerned I should be about [climate change]—on what time scale that might happen, whether that's 100 or 200 years, what societies will be like, what other things are going on with the natural climate. ... I just don't know what the next hundred or 200 years will hold, and whether this will be regarded as an important issue. I just don't know. (Harris)

Curry speaks softly, but she makes the same point that many skeptics make.

Certainly, voices of caution serve a valuable purpose. But if, as many climate scientists tell us, we are approaching a tipping point after which it will be impossible to reverse the warming of the Earth, this kind of reticence could do great—the greatest—harm. If we hope to halt global warming and to mitigate the effects that we are too late to stop, we need broad public agreement. Those who accept climate science's overwhelming judgment are, therefore, exasperated with skeptics, deniers, and even those on the fence, in the same way Ira Glass and Roberta Johnson are frustrated with Erin. Glass asks Erin if there is *anything* a scientist could say that would convince her.

At first, Erin's response might be heartening. As she sums up her reaction to Dr. Johnson's presentation, she sounds not so much like a climate denier as someone who is genuinely befuddled by contradictory claims and evidence. "I get that climate does flux and change," she says, "and that we as people affect the climate. But ... you can find plenty of examples to go with global warming, or climate change, and then a lot to go against it." And she says:

> If I saw both sides of the argument, arguing for both for and against global warming—see those two arguments, completely side by side, laid out, then maybe I could see how it would be true. Or even, more definitely, how it isn't true.

That seems fair enough. Climate science is tough, and an orderly presentation would help.

However, her next observation is the quintessential fly in the ointment. She says:

> I just personally feel like this is kind of almost like evolution. Where you'll have people who will say that, yes, this is fact, and this is what happened. And then there'll be other people who will say, this is theory, it could go one way, it could go the other. And then there'll be the people who say that this is completely untrue.

There we have it, it seems. Erin is listening to religious fundamentalists and placing their conclusions about natural phenomena on an equal plane with those of scientists who submit their work to the ultimate in post-Enlightenment scrutiny: peer-review.

At the end of the show, Glass asks Dr. Johnson, "Once someone is skeptical of this and they see it as a *he said, she said* argument, is it possible to ever get through to them?" With palpable discouragement in her voice, she answers, "Well, we're certainly going to keep trying." She then adds: "I have to remain hopeful that when people have open minds and are equipped to analyze evidence, that they'll come to rational conclusions."

I sympathize. But I also have doubts about the way Dr. Johnson and, it seems, Ira Glass respond to Erin's skepticism. True, Erin has made a damning analogy: Climate denial is a lot like so-called intelligent design (compare Ceccarelli). Both are based on weak or fake science. But I think we also have to ask: Does an irrational conclusion from an observer have to be the product of irrational thought?

Erin does not seem irrational to me. She seems rather intelligent and methodical. Glass and Dr. Johnson would say the same, I'm sure. Still, they are disappointed in her as an audience. They have done their best to persuade her that the facts are the facts, and Erin has not cooperated. Has she fallen short of what we can reasonably expect of an audience? Has she been appropriately skeptical while considering the facts with an open mind? Has she accepted the terms of the debate—that it needs to be settled by the *evidence*?

Although we cannot say for certain what is on Erin's mind, I do feel confident: Erin *believes* she has acted in good faith. She may be predisposed to doubt claims about climate change. However, skepticism is part of what we expect from competent audiences. And if we expect audiences to come to us without predispositions, we will always be disappointed. Yet Erin understands well what is expected of her, and to the best of her ability, she has met those expectations—even if she has left Glass and Dr. Johnson shaking their heads.

The audience to be won

At the time *This American Life* first aired the story with Erin and Dr. Johnson in January 2011, the number of Americans who believed that there was solid evidence for climate change had dropped to 57 percent. It had been 79 percent in 2006 ("Kid Politics"). As of January 2014, the number had risen to 67 percent, which is likely in response to weather events such as Hurricane Sandy ("Climate Change: Key Data Points"). The volatility of public opinion says something about the difficulty of making the argument for climate change. No matter how encouraging spikes in climate change acceptance may be, many people are not very sure about it. Judith Curry may worry about climate scientists' over-confidence. But they face an audience that is slow to stir and quick to backtrack.

Most people believe they are listening with an open mind, exercising ordinary skeptical judgment, and looking—to the best of their ability—at the evidence. Even as they take the issue seriously, they are not ready to panic. Indeed, if the people I meet by chance are at all representative, anthropogenic climate change is a hard, slow sell.

During a particularly warm Midwestern January a couple of years ago, a thirty-ish guy behind a pizza counter told me to "enjoy the weather." I quipped (or tried to), "It's nice if you like the end of the world." He laughed indulgently and said, "Oh, I don't know if I believe all that."

He was not so different from the man I chatted with on a Florida golf course, who commented about heat waves and hurricanes, "It's probably all cyclical, don't you think?" Just as I was poised to brand him as an anti-science dupe, he observed that the Earth had gone through a lot of changes in 4.5 billion years. So my "anti-science" golfing companion knew the age of the Earth off the top of his head.

And he was not so different from a colleague of mine whose daughter has excelled in the natural sciences at a leading university. She asked her daughter what her nerdy friends think about climate change. The report came back: It's real. But a lot of it is probably natural variation.

As it turns out, none of these people—although they may seem quite distinct from each other—are so different from Erin.

Works cited

Blakeslee, Ann M. *Interacting with Audiences: Social Influences on the Production of Scientific Writing.* Mahwah, NJ: Lawrence Erlbaum Associates, 2001. Print.
Ceccarelli, Leah. "Manufactured Scientific Controversy: Science, Rhetoric, and Public Debate." *Rhetoric & Public Affairs* 14.2 (2011): 195–228. Print.
"Climate Change: Key Data Points from Pew Research." Pew Research Center. January 27, 2014. Web. 11 Aug. 2014.

Crowley, Sharon. *Toward a Civil Discourse: Rhetoric and Fundamentalism.* Pittsburgh, PA: U of Pittsburgh, 2006. Print.

Ede, Lisa and Andrea Lunsford. "Audience Addressed/Audience Invoked: The Role of Audience in Composition Theory and Pedagogy." *College Composition and Communication* 35.2 (1984): 155–71. Print.

Elbow, Peter. "Closing My Eyes as I Speak: An Argument for Ignoring Audience." *College English* 49.1 (1987): 50–69. Print.

Harris, Richard. "'Uncertain' Science: Judith Curry's Take on Climate Change." NPR.org. 22 Aug. 2013: n pag. Web. 19 Mar. 2014.

"Kid Politics." *This American Life.* NPR. 17 May 2004. Radio.

Lunsford, Andrea A., John J. Ruszkiewicz, and Keith Walters. *Everything's an Argument: With Readings.* Boston: Bedford/St. Martin's, 2007. Print.

Mann, Michael E. *The Hockey Stick and the Climate Wars: Dispatches from the Front Lines.* New York: Columbia UP, 2012. iBooks file.

Mann, Thomas E., and Norman J. Ornstein. *It's Even Worse than It Looks: How the American Constitutional System Collided with the New Politics of Extremism.* New York: Basic, 2012. Kindle file.

Mathes, J.P. and Dwight W. Stevenson. "Audience Analysis: The Problem and a Solution." *Strategies for Business and Technical Writing.* 4th ed. Ed. Kevin J. Harty. Needham Heights, MA: Allyn and Bacon, 1999. 198–214. Print.

Porter, James E. *Audience and Rhetoric: An Archaeological Composition of the Discourse Community.* Englewood Cliffs, NJ: Prentice Hall, 1992. Print.

Samuelsohn, Darren. "John Shimkus cites Genesis on Climate Change." *Politico.com* 10 Nov. 2010: n. pag. Web. 29 Jan. 2014.

Taylor-Miesle, Heather. "Rush Limbaugh's Uninformed Statement about Christianity and Climate Change." *Huffington Post.* 16 Aug. 2013. n. pag. Web. 6 Jan. 2014.

3   I do believe in science, I do believe in science

Shortly after I first heard Erin's appearance on *This American Life*, I played it for a graduate class on rhetoric and writing. Several of my students were dismayed about the way Ira Glass and Roberta Johnson had "ganged up" on a young woman who was not even 16 years old. They took particular offense at Dr. Johnson's disheartened vow to continue her work in the face of skepticism: "Well, we're certainly going to keep trying. I think there's only so far you can go" ("Kid Politics").

The comment struck me as a harmless expression of frustration. All Dr. Johnson wanted was for people to "have open minds" and to reach "rational conclusions." What could be wrong with that? However, some students thought that she was arrogant and condescending, that she violated the rules of polite argumentation. They pointed out that Erin had, in fact, given Dr. Johnson a fair hearing. She simply disagreed. To ask more of anyone, particularly of a teenager, was just not fair.

In the course of the discussion, I began to think that these students had a point. Adolescence is supposed to be a time when young people learn to think for themselves. Strong-arming them into accepting this or that truth is a poor tactic that teaches the wrong lesson about intellectual self-reliance. But Erin's age was not the whole problem. My students also had something more general in mind: the sacrosanct *right to your own opinion*. And there, I part company with Erin's defenders.

The right to one's own opinion is too often used to justify intransigence. For Roberta Johnson and Ira Glass—and for me—the facts concerning climate change are not a matter of opinion. You can read about them in scientific reports sponsored by the United Nations, in statements from the National Oceanic and Atmospheric Administration, and in other impeccable scientific sources. Or you can do what I do and read about them in the popular press. A passage from *USA Today*:

> The most recent decade was the nation's hottest on record, and 2012 was the hottest single year. The average U.S. temperature has risen 1.5 degrees Fahrenheit since reliable record-keeping began in 1895—80% of that has occurred since 1980. The increase might seem small, but scientists warn that a ripple effect can trigger "tipping points," beyond which the planet may not be able to recover. (Koch)

I often read and hear reports about melting glaciers. I hear experts explain that there is a lag time of about 20 years between the release of greenhouse gases and their effect on global temperatures. I comprehend, at least in a layperson's way, that when the arctic regions melt, additional carbon is released into the air, setting in motion a feedback mechanism that accelerates warming. Ice caps melt. Carbon is released. Ice caps melt even faster.

To the best of my understanding, these facts are beyond dispute. The right to your opinion only begins once you consider all that we, in reality, know. It calls to mind Senator Daniel Moynihan's often-quoted rejoinder, "You may have a right to your own opinion, but you don't have a right to your own facts." I suspect, though, that Moynihan's witticism is not sufficient for the situation we face with climate change

The problem is Moynihan is wrong in the same ways that Roberta Johnson is wrong. They both assume that facts are, in and of themselves, powerful, and that presented with the relevant facts, most of us, with even a modicum of rational consideration, will reach *reasonable* answers to certain sorts of questions. If ever there were an instance where the facts should lead us inexorably toward a single conclusion, the question of anthropogenic climate change is it. Yet they do not.

Even farther off the mark, Moynihan makes a false assertion. The truth is that we *are* entitled to our own facts. That's a large part of what we do when we reason and argue—we decide which "facts" are credible, what weight to give some facts (and not others), and what the implications of those facts might be. How we go about this has everything to do with climate change. It's not a simple question of some of us accepting the facts and others refusing. It's a question of some of us figuring out better than others which claims to credit and which claims—pseudo-facts—to ignore. (That's true no matter who turns out to be right.)

I want to leave Erin behind now with this final observation: She may be the best spokesperson for climate change skepticism that I have encountered. She voices both genuine doubt and a willingness to change her mind, despite an obvious ideological preference. At least, that's what I think I hear in her words and manner.

Let me turn instead to a stand-in for Erin's point of view, seen broadly: *fair-minded skepticism.* For a fair-minded skeptic, the climate change debate looks very much like a *he said, she said* dispute. It's not just a dispute about what's correct and what's not. It's also about what is exaggerated and what is not—about degrees of urgency. I might even call a science-minded friend of mine a fair-minded skeptic. He holds B.A. in geology and believes that climate scientists have made a convincing scientific case. Yet even he suspects that climate scientists' dire warnings are too severe and that we are likely to have more options, for longer, than the so-called climate alarmists say.

The puzzle is how fair-minded skeptics maintain their position in light of a robust scientific consensus, a near unanimous conclusion that climate change is set on a course to destroy most of what humanity relies on and values. A big part of unlocking this puzzle is making an uncomfortable admission that we who support the consensus view are, in some ways, difficult to distinguish from our opponents.

The value of facts

No idea has shaped the Western world in the twentieth and twenty-first centuries more than this cherished Enlightenment inheritance: Doubt and open-mindedness go hand in hand. It is generally agreed that we all should ask the tough questions and that we should, in turn, be willing to change our minds when reason and evidence are genuinely convincing. That intellectual stance is the basis of both the sciences and the humanities—the basis of daily decision-making. It underlies what we teach when we teach students to think and write.

That's why those of us who accept climate change are dismayed when we encounter hard-line climate change skeptics and deniers. For them, it seems that doubt abounds, but its necessary partner, openness, is nowhere to be seen. We know—as journalist Chris Mooney knows—that there is a movement afoot to undermine science on many fronts. And let's be honest, it is mainly afoot in the conservative movement.

Mooney opens his book on science denial with this startler. The conservative alternative website, *Conservapedia.com*, targets nothing less than Einstein's theory of relativity. Relativity denial is news to me, and I find myself wholly unprepared to defend Einstein's work. It is a theory so well established—evidence of genius, after all—that I find it more than a little odd that any non-physicist would feel qualified to refute it or have an interest in refuting it.

That is exactly the reaction Mooney is banking on. He writes:

> You might be thinking that *Conservapedia*'s unabashed denial of relativity is an extreme case. ... If so, I want to ask you to think again. Structurally, the denial of something so irrefutable, the elaborate rationalization of that denial, and above all the refusal to consider the overwhelming body of counterevidence and modify one's view, is something we find all around us today. It's hard to call it rational—and hard to deny it's everywhere. (2–3)

That concern rings true in at least two ways. First, we often hear self-identified conservatives assail scientific "theories." In fact, the word "theory" is often pronounced with derision. Second, it is not just scientific facts under attack. For the extreme political right wing, everything, no matter how demonstrable, is open to dispute. As might be expected, *Conservapedia* disputes the location of Barack Obama's birth ("Barack Hussein Obama").

But denying the theory of relativity still goes pretty far. My aim here is not to expose all of the wild statements made by the wing-nut faction of the lunatic fringe. Rather, I want to note the paradoxical quality of even these extreme arguments. As strange as denialists' arguments may seem, they are virtually always presented in Enlightenment-friendly terms.

That is certainly true of extreme climate-change denial. Consider the "hockey stick" dispute. The "hockey stick" is a graph of average global temperatures from 1000 A.D. until the late twentieth century. In the IPCC's Third Assessment Report, it also showed projections for the twenty-first century ("Climate Change 2001"). The chart was created by mainstream climate scientists Michael Mann, Raymond Bradley, and Malcolm Hughes, and it rests on data that is nothing if not complex (Figure 3.1).

Determining the average temperature of the earth over time is not a simple calculation. You need to account for hemispheric and regional variation. You need to rely not just on recorded temperatures, which are not available for all centuries and places, but also on proxy data. In climate science, proxy data is

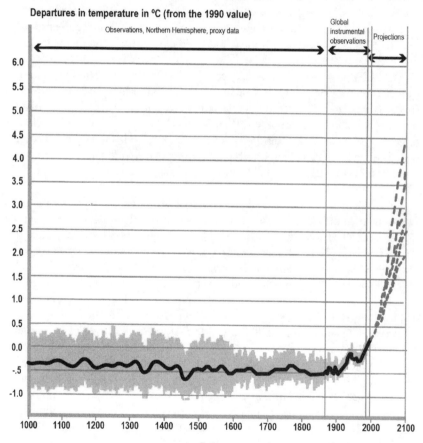

Figure 3.1 The "hockey stick graph." Adapted from *Climate Change 2001: Synthesis Report. A Contribution of Working Groups I, II and III to the Third Assessment Report of the Intergovernmental Panel on Climate Change, Figure SPM–10b.* Cambridge University Press.

produced by analyses of ice cores (very deep cylinders of ice extracted from polar regions), lake and ocean sediments, corals, and tree rings. To produce the most accurate representation of average temperatures, Mann *et al.* undertook a complex statistical weighting of all of this data, using a method called principal component analysis.

The end product of this complex data gathering and statistical work is a surprisingly comprehensible line graph. Imagine a hockey stick lying on its side with the blade to the right. The graph follows a nearly flat horizontal pathway from 1000 C.E. on the left to 1900 C.E. almost all the way to the right, like the shaft. Temperatures have held fairly steady for a long, long time. But then the lines turn sharply upward, like the blade. The chart does represent ranges of uncertainty. However, its general implication is unmistakable. Temperatures are rising dramatically. The earth is getting warmer in a big hurry.

The hockey stick has been a subject of controversy ever since it was first published in 2001. Although skeptics' attacks on climate science in general and on Michael Mann in particular have taken many forms, what I want to point out here is this: The attacks have never included a challenge to the scientific method itself. Rather, skeptics have explicitly appealed to it. In discussing scientific inquiry, the contending sides are not mirror images; they are twins.

Surely the most vocal politician-skeptic is Senator James Inhofe of Oklahoma. Many suspect his motives because of his connections to fossil fuel industries and because of his conservative Christian faith. Yet in *The Great Hoax: How the Global Warming Conspiracy Threatens Your Future*, he defends widely accepted scientific values.

Most strikingly, he quotes at length from Michael Crichton, the now-deceased author of the skeptic's favorite, *State of Fear*:

> In essence, science is nothing more than a method of inquiry. The method says that an assertion is valid—and will be universally accepted—only if it can be reproduced by others, and thereby independently verified. The scientific method is utterly apolitical. The truth in science is verifiable whether you are black or white, male or female, old or young. It's verifiable whether you know the experimenter, or whether you don't. It's verifiable whether you like the results of the study, or you don't. (quoted in Inhofe 249–50)

When it comes to the process of making scientific knowledge, it would seem that we are all in agreement.

Of course, this statement of principle is followed quickly by the accusation that climate scientists have betrayed accepted scientific principles. Inhofe goes on to quote Crichton, who says, "Unfortunately, the converse may also be true: when politics takes precedent over content, it is often because the primacy of independent verification has been abandoned" (250). And in his own words, Inhofe challenges the backbone of scientific objectivity, peer review: "In climate research, the same small group of scientists conducts the majority of the research and peer reviews each other's work. A scientist peer-reviewing a colleague one

year knows that that same colleague may be reviewing their work the next year"
(251). Peer review, he thinks, is just for show.

Such an accusation, levied against scientists at preeminent universities and
government agencies across the world, may seem incredible. But it is not very
different in tone or content from what climate scientists say about skeptics and
deniers. Comparing climate change deniers to earlier defenders of the tobacco
industry, Michael Mann asks:

> Will we hold those who have funded or otherwise participated in the fraudulent
> denial of climate change similarly accountable—those individuals and groups
> who both made and took corporate payoffs for knowingly lying about the threat
> climate change posed to humanity, those who willfully have led the public and
> policymakers astray, and those politicians and media figures who have sought to
> intimidate climate scientists using McCarthyite tactics? (Epilogue)

It's a damning accusation to make. Vituperative tit for vituperative tat.

Likewise, his defense of the science might have been written by Michael
Crichton or, for that matter, *Conservapedia.com*. (I quote only briefly here, but
Mann explains the process of ensuring scientific objectivity at length.)

> Skepticism in the sense of critical consideration of evidence is intrinsic to
> the scientific enterprise. It is inherent in the challenges scientists make of
> each other to back up claims with logical reasoning and, where possible, hard
> data. The scientist must be willing to confront any holes in logic or flaws in
> reasoning noted by fellow scientists and, ultimately, the results must be sub-
> ject to independent replication. … (ch. 6)

He goes on to discuss imperfections in the publication process, but nonetheless
defends science on grounds virtually all of the skeptics and deniers profess to
accept.

In this dispute, I have no trouble deciding who to believe. But fair-minded
skeptics do. And why not? What Mann says about deniers echoes what deniers
say about him and his colleagues. Any cursory Internet search will turn up examples of skeptics, well-known and obscure voices alike, calling into question the
sincerity and competence of scientists. And it will turn up the same accusations
against skeptics.

Consider two customer reviews posted on *Amazon.com*. Each works hard to
establish its credibility—that is, its authority and its belief in standard scientific
methods. Each accuses the other side of the worst kinds of trickery and malfeasance. Each is—for someone with my meager expertise in science and statistics—
factually opaque.

In a review of Michael Mann's *The Hockey Stick and the Climate Wars*,
Shortbloke538 begins by establishing his credentials: "Having a postgrad degree
in Statistics and therefore able to comfortably follow the whole 'Hockey Stick'

affair over the years ..." Then he establishes his own methodological purity by assailing Mann's: "Just for starters, Mann got himself into a whole lot of trouble with Principal Component Analysis (PCA)." For good measure, he attacks Mann's integrity. "Ian Jolliffe, a world-acknowledged leader in the field, had this to say when he was provoked into publicly distancing himself from Mann's methods by Mann falsely claiming he had Jolliffe's support."

Mann is a Distinguished Professor of Meteorology at the University of Pennsylvania. That alone does not guarantee his virtue or the correctness of his conclusions. But it makes the following accusations about his scientific expertise hard to believe. I quote Shortbloke538 at length not because I expect everyone to understand the issues fully but rather because I think many will find themselves, as I do, guessing at what it all means:

> Not only that, Mann made a schoolboy error in his implementation of PCA. When this was discovered by Steve McIntyre, he backtracked on his original claim of having found the "dominant signal" in Northern Hemisphere proxies, to a position of having to depend on an obscure signal explaining less than 10 percent of the proxy data. Few understand the invidious subtlety of Mann's two-stage approach: 1) data mine the proxies for a hockey-stick signal, however faint that signal is, and 2) exploit this unrepresentative signal mercilessly by virtue of a spurious relationship to a (principal component of) highly autocorrelated 20th century temperatures. (Customer reviews of *The Hockey Stick and the Climate Wars*).

I cannot enlighten anyone on this methodological quibble. But I do understand that a scientist who makes a "schoolboy error" must not be a very good scientist. Shortbloke538 concludes: "How this charade passed peer-review I will never understand."

It would be easy to dismiss this customer review as partisan flaming. In fact, I do. But when I do that, do I also need to dismiss, on the same grounds, this disparaging review of A.W. Montford's *The Hockey Stick Illusion: Climategate and the Corruption of Science?* The review is written by Amazon.com user Rob, who begins by explaining Mann and colleagues' data-gathering and statistical methods. He seems to do it well. But, really, how can I say?

> The claim is made that scientists, specifically Mann, were attempting to erase the Medieval Warm Period (MWP). What Mann, Bradley and Hughes were attempting to do is "contain" the MWP ... in other words, they were trying to accumulate enough statistically significant data to "include" the MWP. Their first paper (MBH98) only went back 600 years. The following paper (MBH99) was able to go back 1,000 years, around to the peak of the MWP. The whole impetus of the work was to examine the role of natural variability on global temperature. The "hockey stick" emerged from the data (Customer reviews of *The Hockey Stick Illusion*).

Apparently, Mann and colleagues followed an objective and reasonable scientific procedure.

In the next paragraph, the accusations begin—aimed at Montford, author of *The Hockey Stick Illusion*, and Stephen McIntyre, the statistician who has taken Mann and colleagues to task. Rob says that they "fail to follow very basic tenets of the scientific process. Replication." He casts doubt on their scientific vigor: "They've had over a decade to produce a NH multiproxy reconstruction that presents conclusions that show something different than [Mann *et al.*'s papers] but have failed to do so. Why?" He concludes by trashing both Montford's personal integrity and the intelligence of his readership: "So, while the *Hockey Stick Illusion* is an entertaining conspiracy tome for those who like that sort of reading, it is myopic with regards to its intent and lacking in any real scientific integrity" (Customer reviews of *The Hockey Stick Illusion*).

Can we blame a fair-minded skeptic for thinking that Shortbloke538 and Rob are two sides of the same coin?

Beyond *ad hominem*

It can be difficult to dismiss skeptics' and deniers' arguments because they are often quite skilled in presenting them. James Inhofe's *The Greatest Hoax* is fact-filled and footnoted. Chapter Four alone has 222 citations. Inhofe takes pains to establish the reliability of the authorities he cites: MIT climate scientist Richard Lindzer, Dr. S. Fred Singer, formerly an atmospheric scientist at the University of Virginia [the same institution that employed Michael Mann before he moved to Pennsylvania State University], and Hans Von Storch, a prominent German researcher with the GKSS Institute for Coastal Research. All of his sources and authorities are open to question—and are, indeed, questioned. But a fair-minded skeptic could be forgiven for saying, "If it walks like a duck…"

Climate-change discourse does not want for name-calling, it is true. It is precisely the kind of discourse that is undesirable—so it would seem—in a scientific dispute. But it also matters what kind of mud is slung. By and large, the names called and the slurs hurled have to do with corruption of the scientific process. Inhofe accuses Al Gore of being a green profiteer and says, "Don't feel too sorry for Al Gore. A billion dollars is a lot of comfort" (introduction). But, then, it is routine to dismiss skeptics' arguments on the basis of their political and financial connections. If it seems uncivil for Inhofe to speak of "phony science" (introduction), it is not far different in tone from Al Gore's statement on *60 Minutes* that climate change skeptics are "almost like the ones who still believe that the moon landing was staged in a movie lot in Arizona and those who believe the world is flat" ("The Gore Campaign").

It is far more worrisome, however, when the *ad hominem* progresses from mere name-calling into political and legal assaults. In 2006, Representative Joe Barton, Republican of Texas, launched a rogue congressional investigation into Michael Mann's funding sources, scientific associations, and data. In 2010, Mann was attacked by the National Center for Public Policy Research (funded by the right-wing Scaife Foundation), which tried to have his NSF (National Science Foundation) grants revoked. Another Scaife-funded organization, the Commonwealth Foundation, pressured Pennsylvania State University to fire Mann because of accusations of wrongdoing in the so-called Climategate scandal. (Mann ch. 10)

Note to self: When you try to save the world, not everyone is grateful.

Works cited

Climate Change 2001: IPCC Third Assessment Report. "Summary for Policymakers." 7: 33–34. Web. 11 Aug. 2014.

Conservapedia.com. "Barack Hussein Obama" Web. 12 Feb. 2014.

Inhofe, James M. *The Greatest Hoax: How the Global Warming Conspiracy Threatens Your Future.* Washington, D.C.: WND, 2012. iBooks file.

"Kid Politics." *This American Life.* NPR. 17 May 2004. Radio.

Koch, Wendy. "Why You Should Sweat Climate Change." *USA Today.* 1 Mar. 2013. Usatoday.com. 29 Jan. 2014.

Mann, Michael E. *The Hockey Stick and the Climate Wars: Dispatches from the Front Lines.* New York: Columbia UP, 2012. iBooks file.

Mooney, Chris. *The Republican Brain: The Science of Why They Deny Science and Reality.* Hoboken, NJ: Wiley, 2012. Kindle file.

Buzz. Customer review of *The Hockey Stick Illusion: Climategate and the Corruption of Science.* Amazon.com. 8 June 2012. n. pag. Web. 2 Jan. 2014.

Shortbloke538. Customer review of *The Hockey Stick and the Climate Wars: Dispatches from the Front Lines.* Amazon.com. 12 April 2012. n. pag. Web. 2 Jan. 2014.

"The Gore Campaign." *60 Minutes,* CBS. 27 Mar. 2008. Television.

4 Who do you doubt?

Here is one way to describe the climate change debate.

In one corner, reasonable scientists and policymakers say that human activity is causing dangerous climate change. They evaluate the facts in the cool light of scientific reason and accept the unavoidable conclusions. In the other corner, climate deniers say that the science is not settled and claim to be relying on scientific studies that the so-called consensus refuses to acknowledge. But, in reality, they are fundamentalist Christians who do not fully accept the whole idea of science, or they are cronies of energy companies who are really after a profit. In short, the climate change deniers are benighted or bought or both.

Much of that may be a fair description, at least, of the most prominent public voices. But even if it is, it doesn't account for the broad influence of climate change skepticism or the lukewarm acceptance among many who accept, generally speaking, what climate scientists have told us, yet suspect that the threat is exaggerated or misstated. It doesn't explain how so many people can remain unconvinced or neutral when faced with a crisis as potentially cataclysmic as climate change.

Think for a moment about the scale and urgency of scientists' and environmentalists' warnings. For example, here is what the eminent scientist James Lovelock says:

> Humanity, wholly unprepared by its humanist traditions, faces its greatest trial. The acceleration of the climate change now under way will sweep away the comfortable environment to which we are adapted. ... [N]othing so severe has happened since the long hot period at the start of the Eocene, fifty-five million years ago, when the change was larger than that between the ice age and the nineteenth century and lasted for 200,000 years. (7)

That is a dire prediction indeed. Nevertheless, it is not inconsistent with predictions routinely made by climate scientists and activists.

The political scholar and environmentalist David Orr writes:

> With another degree or so of warming, the changes will be unmistakable: traditional winters will be mostly a memory, food prices will rise sharply,

forest fires will be more frequent, and many species will disappear. Maple syrup will no longer be made in Vermont. With still another degree, coastal cities like New Orleans, Miami, and Baltimore will eventually be flooded, the Everglades will disappear, Appalachian forests will be replaced by scrub trees and grasses, and a great human migration away from coasts and mid-continental regions will have begun. (2–3)

And that's not all. He warns us: "Climate change, like the threat of nuclear annihilation, puts all that humanity has struggled to achieve—our cultures, art, music, literatures, cities, institutions, customs, religions, and histories, as well as our posterity—at risk" (4).

To dismiss such warnings would require something extraordinary. It would seem to require more than just religious convictions that, after all, have little directly to do with climate science. It would require more than short-term profit motives, no matter how large the profit. Yet a significant number of people—even those who do not strongly doubt the science—greet these catastrophic predictions with a shrug. What I often find incomprehensible about these easy dismissals is not ignorance or even corruption, but the underlying calm.

Consider this statement by United States Representative Joe Barton of Texas, who is no fence-sitter in the climate change debate—who is, in fact, a great enemy of climate science and environmentalism. Even as he foregrounds his Biblical and energy-industry perspective, he strikes a relatively moderate tone. In a House subcommittee hearing, he says:

> I would point out that people like me who support hydrocarbon development don't deny that climate is changing. I think you can have an honest difference of opinion of what's causing that change without automatically being either all in that it's all because of mankind or it's all just natural. I think there's a divergence of evidence. I would point out that if you're a believer in the Bible, one would have to say the Great Flood is an example of climate change and that certainly wasn't because mankind had overdeveloped hydrocarbon energy. (Kiene)

Although Barton raises a literalist Biblical view and an industry loyalty that many people in the consensus find disturbing, he also makes what might *sound* like a reasonable point. The climate can indeed change for reasons other than human-induced emissions of carbon. Furthermore, when it comes to humans' role in climate change, you don't have to say that it's "all because of mankind or it's all just natural." It is just a difference of opinion to him, like many other disputes that arise day in and day out. It all sounds so calm and fair-minded.

Of course, Barton is merely stating what climate scientists have said. Scientists do not claim that all climate change is caused by humans; they claim that the climate is changing more and faster than can be attributed to natural cycles alone. So, either through ignorance or guile, Barton has misstated the controversy.

Here's what ought to disturb us more than his wrong-headedness or his dubious loyalties: In one important respect, we can trust Barton. And we can trust more moderate climate change skeptics in the same way, even more so. They say they are not convinced that climate change is an existential threat to us, and they genuinely doubt that people are primarily responsible for the Earth's recent warming. That has to be the case, doesn't it? No one could take that position otherwise.

But how can anyone remain calm, knowing what we know? Is there really that much room for doubt?

The doubting game

We shouldn't take too much pride in our doubting habits. Doubt is easy, and it makes us feel smart. Belief is much harder. When we believe, we have to hand intellectual power to someone else. *I'm right* is much easier to say than *you're right*. Or so some very smart people have said.

In his 1974 classic, *Modern Dogma and the Rhetoric of Assent*, Wayne Booth tackled the problem of disbelief. Recall that the late 1960s were a time of angry protests over the Vietnam War. Prevalent youth mottos virtually ruled out open dialogue: *Don't trust anyone over thirty. Never trust the establishment.* Booth observed accurately, in my opinion, that this impasse could never be resolved until trust was established. That was difficult to do because each side held the unshakable view that no matter what they said, the other side had ulterior motives.

So Booth laid out a scheme for setting aside suspicion or, as he put it more often, setting aside doubt. The trick, he says, is to reverse our habitual skepticism, which means, in varying degrees, accepting all that it is not reasonable to doubt. In a similar way, Peter Elbow advises college writers to abandon the "doubting game," sometimes called critical thinking, which is "the disciplined practice of trying to be as skeptical and analytic as possible with every idea we encounter. ... [to] discover hidden contradictions, bad reasoning, or other weaknesses in them." He recommends instead the "believing game," which "asks us to scrutinize unfashionable or even repellent ideas for hidden virtues" ("The Believing Game" 2).

Booth and Elbow both envision a nicer world. And in a way, we who support the consensus view have followed Booth's and Elbow's advice. True, climate change is precisely the kind of question for which methodical doubt is most useful. We want scientists to analyze and scrutinize and be difficult to convince. But we are not scientists, and once scientists' doubts have been satisfied, it makes sense for the rest of us to play the believing game—despite the abhorrent conclusions scientists have reached. All we ask of skeptics is that they set aside unreasonable doubt.

In reality, most of us are ill-equipped to judge the facts about climate change and are, therefore, always at risk of believing the wrong thing. We may have seen images of melting polar regions and read far too many news reports of extreme weather. Those things we understand. Yet the in-depth scientific case lies well outside our own expertise, and so we have to rely on belief.

This is not such an unusual spot to be in. A lot of what I read on any number of topics is, to say the least, not my specialty. So, I make judgments about them in much the way that Paul Krugman makes judgments. Asked by Chris Hayes how people should distinguish good arguments from bad ones, Krugman says:

> That's a hard issue. I mean, in fact, what do I do on issues that are—I don't know—the technical stuff. I look for style. I look for people who seem to be actually looking at evidence. I look for people who've been willing on occasion to admit that they made a mistake in the past. I look for some sign that a person is actually seriously studying as opposed to just spouting a public line. (*Up*)

Krugman plays the believing game, but not haphazardly. He applies his judgment not just to arguments themselves but also to the manner of argumentation. Not just logos. Also ethos.

If sound arguments were all dramatically different in style from false ones, that method might do. I want to suggest, though, that this procedure is difficult to apply broadly and may be particularly problematic with respect to climate change. How do we—those who support the consensus—know we're not just playing a version of the old TV game show *Who Do You Trust?* And if we are, why should we think that we navigate the discursive world better than skeptics and deniers do?

Surely, from time to time, we all err either on the side of credulity or on the side of disbelief. But since the climate change debate has a particular bone to pick with skepticism, let's consider for a moment the things that might justify excessive doubt in a world that gives us too few clues about what information and arguments are genuinely reliable.

A *sea of bullshit*

When people have an obvious motivation—self-interest, ideology—it makes sense to exercise doubt. Many people suspect climate scientists and people who support them of being zealots—blinded by a particular point of view, willing to say whatever it takes.

Even the leading climate scientist Stephen Schneider (who died in 2010) once commented, to his regret I don't doubt, about the difficulty of talking about climate change to the public:

> [Like] most people, [scientists would] like to see the world a better place, which in this context translates into our working to reduce the risk of potentially disastrous climatic change. To do that we need to get some broad based support, to capture the public's imagination. That, of course, entails getting

loads of media coverage. So we have to offer up scary scenarios, make simplified, dramatic statements, and make little mention of any doubts we might have. This 'double ethical bind' we frequently find ourselves in cannot be solved by any formula. Each of us has to decide what the right balance is between being effective and being honest. I hope that means being both. (Quoted in Mann ch. 5)

Schneider expresses with remarkable candor what happens when important arguments need be sold rather than simply told. Once science leaves the safety of academic journals and enters the public sphere, it swims in the same sea with other public discourse. Would I be wrong to say that we are all afloat in a discursive ocean of mistakes, exaggerations, and outright lies? If I am wrong, how far wrong?

For example, when it comes to most marketing communication, no sentient American bothers to expect the truth. What we expect is bullshit, which is a form of lying that is not quite synonymous with telling falsehoods. Consider the recent book *Your Call Is Important to Us: The Truth About Bullshit*. The title strikes a chord because we have all spent long minutes on the telephone, being reminded by a recording that although no one will actually talk to us, our call is a high priority.

That's not quite a lie. I don't doubt that my call is "important" to [fill in the blank]. But only in the sense that *all* the details of any operation are important. And so I give the voice on the telephone a *truth discount*. From marketers, none of us ever asks for the whole truth, just a grain of it. We apply a truth discount when a menu touts a "famous" specialty. That trope is so familiar that the Cowbell Diner in New Orleans brags about its "locally world famous burger." "World famous burger" may be a factual falsehood. Yet it's not the factual discrepancy that makes it bullshit. It's what Harry Frankfurt identifies as the key to bullshit: misrepresentation of the self. Marketers don't always lie about their products (though sometimes they do). But they virtually always misrepresent themselves to one degree or another.

As I composed the previous paragraph, I noticed a magazine sitting on the chair beside me. In it is a glossy ad run by Siemens for its medical equipment. It pictures a father reading to his daughter. She looks up at him, smiling adoringly. The headline reads: "More healthcare stories with happier endings. Siemens technology is helping to give families the answers they need, when they need them." I do not doubt it. Without Siemens, many people would be sicker than they are and would depart the Earth sooner than they might otherwise. Surely, Siemens is a company filled with good people whose aim is to do good.

But the ad is still a particular kind of self-representation—a selective one and perhaps even a deceptive one. At least, I begin to suspect that when I read *Time* magazine's healthcare exposé, which shines a light on the excessive profit-taking of hospitals, pharmaceutical companies, and medical equipment manufacturers, including Siemens. Among other things, Siemens makes CT scanners, which are used as a "great defense" against being sued (Brill 24), according to one hospital CEO. One manufacturer reports a 75.1 percent gross margin on its devices, which compares well with, for example, Apple's 40 percent gross margin on its computers and devices (Brill 36).

We should not make the mistake of thinking Siemens stands alone in selective image-building in advertisements; nothing could be more common. Neither should we uncritically accept *Time* magazine's critique of Siemens. However, the contrast between Siemens' self-representation and the picture of the company presented by *Time* is striking. Rightly or wrongly, the contrast plants a seed of doubt, and it is relevant to the climate change debate. It is not just commerce that we are invited to doubt. To profit excessively (as some claim) on medical equipment is a corruption of science. It is only a few short steps from suspecting Siemens of bullshitting us to suspecting climate scientists of doing the same.

In fact, as John Schaeffer and I have discussed, in many areas of communication—academic writing being no exception—we make allowances in varying degrees for professional bullshitting. Bullshitting ranges from benign self-promotion to utter fraud. It can involve factual untruths. And it can be factually impeccable and yet present a false picture of the bullshitter.

One thing routine bullshitting surely does to all of us: It conditions us to expect something less than complete truthfulness from almost anyone. In this atmosphere of bullshit, is it unreasonable for us to doubt what climatologists and environmentalists say? Is it possible that they represent themselves as truth-tellers when, in fact, what they really want is to advance an agenda? Is it possible, as Stephen Schneider once admitted, that they feel justified in spouting "scary scenarios" and resorting to "simplified, dramatic statements" and failing to mention "any doubts we might have"? Is it possible that climate scientists and their adherents are bullshitting us?

Nonfiction's tortured relationship with the truth

We usually have an expectation of truth and accuracy from all kinds of nonfiction sources—television news, newspapers, magazines, history books, memoirs. Or perhaps it would be better to say: We feel we have a right to expect the truth, even as we also expect disappointment. The old adage tells us, *Don't believe everything you read.* Most of us understand that the "facts" we encounter in the media every day are subject to revision and that some should be revised, but, for reasons having to do with human beings' inherent imperfection, they never are.

Libby Lester recounts one factual slip-up that still casts its shadow over climate change reporting and debate: the question of polar bear populations (61–62). The polar bear has become the poster animal for the prospect of mass extinctions due to climate change. Claims about their numbers are often in dispute; accusations of falsification are often made with great adamance; and it remains difficult for the public to know what the truth of the matter is. Polar bear populations are affected by things other than climate change, such as hunting and hunting bans. Evidently, for valid reasons, it is difficult for scientists to count them accurately.

Because of this overheated rhetorical atmosphere, what might seem to be a small error in reporting turns out to be important. In 2006, *The New York Times* said in a story about polar bears hunted by indigenous people, "Other experts see a healthier population. They note that there are more than 20,000 polar bears roaming the Arctic, compared to as few as 5,000 40 years ago" (Lester 61). Over time, that claim has been repeated in numerous media stories (with some variation in the numbers), including in a *Wall Street Journal* article five years later.

The problem is that the claim is just not accurate. A CNN reporter tracked down the scientists who made what they called a "guess-timate," now more than half a century old. They repudiated the number 5,000 and said their guess-timate was 20,000 to 25,000, which would indicate a relatively stable polar bear population. We all know, or should know, that errors like this one find their way into media reports and that we should be cautious. It has always been so.

Nonetheless, the credibility of nonfiction sources seems to be on shakier ground than ever. I do not mean only that many news sources brazenly promote their ideological biases—Fox News, MSNBC, *The Huffington Post*, and *The Washington Times*. I do not mean only that "the media" has been the subject of relentless character assassination from the conservative movement because of its purported "liberal bias." Of course, these things have contributed to the declining reputation of journalism. But in the past couple of decades, all manner of fact-based discourse has suffered highly publicized blows to their credibility.

I refer, in part, to a steady stream of plagiarism and fakery cases. To cite just a few: Stephen Glass, faked stories for the *New Republic* in 1998[1]; Patricia Smith, faked stories for the *Boston Globe* in 1998[2]; Stephen Ambrose, accused of plagiarism in a history book in 2002[3]; Doris Kearns Goodwin, accused of plagiarism in a history book in 2002[4]; Jayson Blair, faked stories for *The New York Times* in 2003[5]; Rick Bragg, misrepresented his role in reporting a *New York Times* story in 2003[6]; Fareed Zakaria, accused of plagiarizing portions of his *Washington Post* column in 2012[7]; and Fox News commentator Juan Williams, accused of plagiarism in 2013[8].

Memoirs have been faked again and again: James Frey was exposed for faking his memoir *A Million Little Pieces* in 2006 (the book had been an Oprah Book Club selection, and the revelation of fakery brought about a dramatic confrontation between Frey and Winfrey)[9]; Herman Rosenblat was exposed for faking his holocaust memoir *Angel at the Fence* in 2008 (another Oprah Book Club selection, just two years after the Frey debacle)[10]; and Greg Mortenson was accused of fabricating substantial parts of *Three Cups of Tea* in 2011[11].

I have made no attempt to provide a comprehensive list of infractions or to adjudicate any particular accusation. I only want to remind us that accusations of such misconduct are routine. We may find it comforting that in all of the cases above, the newspapers, book publishers, and broadcasters fired or reprimanded the perpetrators. But we have, nonetheless, been made aware—persistently and often shockingly—that apparently reliable publications are too often, in one way or another, megaphones for liars and fakes. We cannot un-ring that bell.

Whatever the causes for mistrust of the so-called "media," the trend toward mistrust is clear. And it has only been exacerbated by the decline of reportorial news and the accompanying growth of opinion. The Pew Research Center's *State of the News Media Annual Report for 2010* says that "72% of Americans feel now most news sources are biased in their coverage" ("Major Trends").

I am tempted to take this a step further. The trend toward opinion is indisputable, but there is also a philosophical debate in progress that calls into question the very necessity of facts. It's especially evident in what is called, mostly in academic circles, but elsewhere too, "creative nonfiction." The idea is roughly this: Some pieces of nonfiction writing should probably be factually accurate—such as in traditional newspaper and magazine articles. But creative nonfiction may be fact-based, but it needn't be fact bound. In that arena, Truth is important but not necessarily truthfulness.

Mike Daisey used that defense when he was caught with his facts off in *The Agony and Ecstasy of Steve Jobs*. His account of working conditions in China was presented originally as a stage monologue. When the passage was excerpted on *This American Life* in 2012, it was exposed for its numerous fabrications, which led host Ira Glass to confront Mike Daisey on the air à la Winfrey-Frey. Their conversation was not so much a mea culpa moment as an uncomfortable debate about the role of fact in conveying Truth.

Daisey claimed his story was "true," even though, as it turned out, he never saw armed guards outside a Chinese factory, never spoke with 12-year-old workers in a factory making Apple products, never met with labor activists at a Chinese Starbucks, and so on. Daisey argued that the theater—even when it claims to be telling the truth—adheres to a different standard from journalism or, for that matter, ordinary life. Strict factual accuracy, he said, is not useful or expected ("Retraction").

Well, perhaps that is so in the theater. Perhaps. But how about nonfiction feature stories in reputable magazines? An extended discussion of that problem is presented in John D'Agata and Jim Fingal's *The Lifespan of a Fact*. Fingal was once assigned to fact check a magazine article written by D'Agata, an article that centers on the suicide of Levi Presley, a teenager who jumped from the top of the Stratosphere Hotel and Casino on July 13, 2002. Fingal discovered numerous—innumerable might be a better word—factual errors and misrepresentations.

The debate between D'Agata and Fingal is presented as what appears to be a series of e-mail exchanges between the two men. Each factual dispute is dissected with (sometimes rather stunning) candor. But even this apparent peek into the inner workings of fact-checking draws us into a factual hall of mirrors. One of the conceits of the book is that it is not a candid revelation at all; rather, it is a *post hoc* conversation constructed by the authors. Nowhere does the book explicitly claim to be a transcript of anything. You are not lied to *per se*. You are simply misled, bullshitted, fooled. Several reviewers credulously described the book as a real-time transcript of D'Agata's and Fingal's e-mails. It never occurred to them to doubt that the book was not what it appeared to be.

In the exchanges, D'Agata argues that because he is not a journalist, he is not required to be completely factual. If he thinks it sounds better, he can say that a car was purple rather than pink or say that there were 34 strip clubs in Las Vegas rather than 31.

If he wants to achieve a certain emotional effect, he can also say that all of the following events occurred in Las Vegas on the day of Levi Presley's suicide: lap dancing was temporarily banned; the oldest bottle of Tabasco hot sauce was found underneath an old bar called Buckets of Blood; a Mississippi woman defeated a chicken (named Ginger) at tic-tac-toe; five people died from two types of cancer; four people died of heart attacks; three died of strokes; there were two suicides by gunshot; and there was one suicide by hanging.

It was quite a day in Las Vegas—if you believe what D'Agata writes.

But fact-checker Fingal rejects much of this. There were eight heart attacks, not four. The third suicide was not from hanging; it was from jumping off a building. The Mississippi woman defeated the chicken at tic-tac-toe more than a month after Presley's suicide. The bottle of Tabasco was discovered two weeks before Presley's suicide. And it wasn't found in Las Vegas but rather in Virginia City, 450 miles away. The bar was called the Boston Saloon, not Buckets of Blood. And it wasn't Tabasco brand hot sauce; it was Frank's RedHot Sauce (15-17).

That's quite a few factual discrepancies in a mere 188 words. But D'Agata is unconcerned. He says that none of these discrepancies undermines the truth of his piece and that adhering more closely to the details would be too clunky for the kind of writing he means to do. Moreover, he insists that if readers knew that he'd taken these liberties, they wouldn't mind—they are not concerned with strict factuality.

I am reminded of Sissela Bok's book on lying. She points out the problem of asymmetry. Sometimes people feel justified in telling benevolent lies. Many healthcare professionals, for example, think it's not only ethical but also compassionate to mislead terminal patients in order to give them hope. But patients who've been misled tend not to agree (225-41). In that same way, I suspect D'Agata would find his readers do not want to grant him the leeway he thinks they might.

D'Agata may not be typical of all nonfiction writers. However, he is not *rara avis*. We live in a world where truth and facts are more than ever negotiable. And now is probably as good a time as any to mention a factual discrepancy in this very book. When I listed factual lapses in the first 188 words of D'Agata's essay, I actually inserted an error that D'Agata did not make. To me, the paragraph seemed to lose some punch when I left it out. The error I attributed to him—it is actually very small. Besides, the overall Truth of the paragraph remains intact.

I was sure you wouldn't mind.

Doubting in science, doubting of science

Trust in the press may be on the decline, but—paradoxically—when it comes to reports about science, I suspect we often read press reports with naïve credulity. A lot of people do understand that press reports leave out the nuances and hedges that scientists build into their professional publications. I certainly do. Nevertheless, I read hopefully about each new discovery concerning Alzheimer's disease, cancer, and more. This credulous reading is a part of what Jacques Lyotard once called the grand narrative of science, a narrative of inexorable progress and wondrous breakthroughs.

Indeed, popular accounts of science can encourage an uncomplicated faith in the story of scientific progress, which is—to use an old cliché—swallowed whole. Dale Jamieson attributes this naïvety to widespread scientific ignorance. He points out that only 28 percent of Americans are knowledgeable enough about science to read *The New York Times* science section and that there is "little awareness of the fact that scientific authority comes in degrees and that science generally advances incrementally" (ch. 2).

If the story of scientific progress is too often uncritically accepted, that is not the only problem we face. There is a competing narrative that we read perhaps just as naïvely—a story of failure and fraud. It is standard fare for the news media to expose the shortcomings of scientific research. Some stories involve dubious claims, such as the famed cold fusion announcement made by two University of Utah scientists in the late 1980s. Others are stories of faked data that reveal some scientists' unbounded personal ambition.

For example, in 2013, *The New York Times Magazine* ran a story about Diederik Stapel, an academic "con man." Stapel was an academic superstar who published studies of human behavior in prestigious venues such as *Science* until it was discovered that he had fabricated data in numerous studies. Stapel's lapses were not small. They make good stories, too. In one faked study, the experimental design called for the participants to be rewarded with M&Ms. But since Stapel never performed the actual study, he ate most of the M&Ms himself (Bhattacharjee).

There is more than just a quirky story at stake here—at least, according to *The New York Times Magazine*. The article describes Stapel's cheating as egregious, yet part of a larger problem. It mentions Hwang Woo-suk, the South Korean researcher who made the news for faking data about his world-famed stem-cell research. It mentions Marc Hauser, the evolutionary biologist who resigned from Harvard in 2011 for faking data. Then, it makes a rather broad claim:

> Each case of research fraud that's uncovered triggers a similar response from scientists. First disbelief, then anger, then a tendency to dismiss the perpetrator as one rotten egg in an otherwise-honest enterprise. But the scientific misconduct that has come to light in recent years suggests at the very least that the number of bad actors in science isn't as insignificant as many would like to believe. And considered from a more cynical point of view, *figures like Hwang and Hauser are*

*not outliers so much as one end on a continuum of dishonest behaviors that extend
from the cherry-picking of data to fit a chosen hypothesis—which many researchers
admit is commonplace—to outright fabrication.* (Bhattacharjee, emphasis added)

In other words, you might plausibly maintain your belief in the scientific method,
but you should not necessarily trust scientists.

Interestingly, Stapel's self-justification (to the extent that he attempts one)
is strikingly reminiscent of John D'Agata's. The reporter who interviewed him
recalls:

Several times in our conversation, Stapel alluded to having a fuzzy, postmod-
ernist relationship with the truth, which he agreed served as a convenient
fog for his wrongdoings. "It's hard to know the truth," he said. "When some-
body says, 'I love you,' how do I know what it really means?" (Bhattacharjee)

Moreover, like D'Agata, Stapel saw the advantages of presenting a clean, force-
ful story, rather than adhering closely to facts. The article describes his slide into
fraud this way:

In his early years of research—when he supposedly collected real experimental data—Stapel wrote papers laying out complicated and messy rela-
tionships between multiple variables. He soon realized that journal editors
preferred simplicity. "They are actually telling you: 'Leave out this stuff.
Make it simpler,'" Stapel told me. Before long, he was striving to write ele-
gant articles. (Bhattacharjee)

Of course, scientists would have us believe that editors' tastes play no part in the
rigorous process of peer review.

The cumulative effect of stories like Stapel's, along with other stories that
undermine confidence in science, cannot help but be negative. Scientific progress
is often cast as the correction of a mistake that science has made.

Consider *The New York Times* article titled "Mice Fall Short as Test Subjects for
Some of Humans' Deadly Ills." The article reports that H. Shaw Warren, Ronald
W. Davis, and their colleagues discovered that at least for sepsis and for a few other
diseases, mouse studies were not helpful but in fact were misleading (Kolata). This
news is important in medical research. Mouse studies have long been an essential
component of this kind of inquiry. In fact, it is difficult to publish medical research
that does not include mouse studies. And now we hear that they are not valid?

The *Times* reports on resistance from the scientific community. Warren and
Davis's article was rejected by *Science* and *Nature*. An editor from *Science* is
quoted as saying that "the most common response [of peer reviewers] was, 'It
has to be wrong. I don't know why it is wrong, but it has to be wrong.'" Then, in
a final flourish, the *Times* story makes it sound as if—though it had just quoted
experts who called the study "stunning," "amazing," and a "game changer"—we

should have suspected it all along: "Yet there was always one major clue that mice might not really mimic humans in this regard: it is very hard to kill a mouse with a bacterial infection. Mice need a million times more bacteria in their blood than what would kill a person" (Kolata).

So much for science. Of course, some online readers say that the article over-simplifies to the point of misrepresenting the studies it reports on. But how are we to know?

Some popular articles call into question the very foundation of science itself: the experimental method. *The New Yorker* reports on what it tentatively terms "the decline effect." In this phenomenon, scientists find themselves unable, over time, to replicate (or to replicate to the same degree) important scientific findings. *The New Yorker* writes:

> [All] sorts of well-established, multiply confirmed findings have started to look increasingly uncertain. It's as if our facts were losing their truth: claims that have been enshrined in textbooks are suddenly unprovable. This phenomenon doesn't yet have an official name, but it's occurring across a wide range of fields, from psychology to ecology. (Lehrer)

The phenomenon is apparently real enough, and it applies to scientific findings that seem inarguably objective, such as the relative symmetry of a bird's tail feathers. *The New Yorker* issues this warning:

> For many scientists, the [decline] effect is especially troubling because of what it exposes about the scientific process. If replication is what separates the rigor of science from the squishiness of pseudoscience, where do we put all these rigorously validated findings that can no longer be proved? (Lehrer)

Indeed.

There are plausible explanations for the decline effect—regression toward the mean (the tendency for statistics to level out when the samples become larger) and simple human error. Just as troubling as findings that cannot be replicated is the reluctance of the scientific establishment to correct itself. The Australian biologist Michael Jennions is quoted as follows: "This is a very sensitive issue for scientists. You know, we're supposed to be dealing with hard facts, the stuff that's supposed to stand the test of time. But when you see these trends you become a little more skeptical of things" (Lehrer).

Again, indeed.

To make matters worse, *The New Yorker* highlights the reluctance of scientific journals to publish studies that contradict established findings. The journals, it says, have a bias toward positive results. They simply are not as interested in studies that show little or no statistical significance as they are in studies that do.

To make matters worse yet, the article that raises this new doubt about the scientific method was written by Jonah Lehrer, who received a good deal of media attention for faking Bob Dylan quotes in his book *Imagine*, which had to be recalled by its publisher (Kinney).

Whether or not it is reported with perfect fidelity, all of this criticism of science originates with scientists. Without their candor, none of this would be known. As Gilbert and Mulkay showed us in the mid-1980s, scientific progress can be messy, and scientists know that. That is why they so often reassure us that eventually, the truth will win the day. Gilbert and Mulkay call this the "Truth Will Out Device" (TWOD).

But still.

The decline of the scientific fact

Even if we place our trust in the scientific process, with all of its slow messiness, we must still address the question of "the scientific fact." Who can say how much effect postmodern critiques of discourse have had on the world at large? But if they have had any effect at all, it has not redounded to the benefit of science. For the past three decades or more, postmodernists have argued, more or less, that all of the things we think are objective facts are really ephemeral constructions. That claim has been vigorously applied to science.

Notably, in the late 1970s, Bruno Latour and Lawrence Woolgar advanced a complex, subtle, and influential argument about scientific facts. Google Scholar records more than 8,000 citations on their fly-on-the-wall description of how science works, *Laboratory Life: The Social Construction of Scientific Facts*. They do not deny the efficacy of science. However, they do work hard to reveal the processes by which facts are constructed: the literary inscriptions, the unguarded conversations, the temporal sequences, and so on. They write, "'Reality' cannot be used to explain why a statement becomes a fact, since it is only after it has become a fact that the effect of reality is obtained" (180). To paraphrase (clumsily perhaps): Scientists do not recognize scientific reality and then name it; they produce a name and then convince others through a series of discursive processes that the name corresponds to reality. That description is not supposed to be a refutation of science; it is supposed to complicate what we mean by "fact."

Yet one law of nature that cannot be disputed is the law of unintended consequences. It has not escaped everyone's notice that a version of those same sorts of arguments now animates science denial, including the denial of climate change.

That phenomenon caused Bruno Latour to write in *Critical Inquiry*:

> Entire Ph.D. programs are still running to make sure that good American kids are learning the hard way that facts are made up, that there is no such thing as natural, unmediated, unbiased access to truth … while dangerous extremists are using the very same argument of social construction to destroy hard-won evidence that could save our lives. Was I wrong to participate in the invention of this field known as science studies? Is it enough to say that we did not really mean what we meant? Why does it burn my tongue to say

that global warming is a fact whether you like it or not? Why can't I simply say that the argument is closed for good? (Quoted in Bérubé)

Postmodern thinker Michael Bérubé responds simply: "Why, indeed? Why not say, definitively, that anthropogenic climate change is real, that vaccines do not cause autism, that the Earth revolves around the Sun, and that Adam and Eve did not ride dinosaurs to church?"

Not many are as clever as Bérubé, but many have said much the same thing. The problem is, when you say that, you have also said, with or without justification: *My critique of science's epistemology is legitimate, and my opponent's is not.*

Notes

1 According to *The New York Times*, *The New Republic* investigated articles contributed to the magazine by Stephen Glass and "found that Mr. Glass had completely fabricated six articles and had manufactured material in parts of 21 other articles." Pogrebin, Robin. "Rechecking a Writer's Facts, A Magazine Uncovers Fiction: Magazine Finds Writer's Fabrications." *The New York Times*. 12 June 1998: A1.

2 According to *The New York Times*, Patricia Smith "was caught fabricating quotes and characters in her *Boston Globe* columns." Goldberg, Carey. "The Lack of Truth Brings a Bounty of Consequences." *The New York Times*. 20 June 1998: A6.

3 According to *The New York Times*, Stephen Ambrose "acknowledged that his current best seller, 'The Wild Blue,' inappropriately borrowed words and phrases from a book by the historian Thomas Childers, 'The Wings of Morning.'" Kirkpatrick, David D. "As Historian's Fame Grows, So Do Questions on Methods." *The New York Times*. 11 January 2002: A1.

4 *The New York Times* reported, "In January, Ms. [Doris Kearns] Goodwin acknowledged that in 1987 her publisher, Simon & Schuster, paid another author to settle accusations of plagiarism in her book 'The Fitgeralds and the Kennedys.' Then, acting to pre-empt new accusations by Philip Nobile, a journalist, Ms. Goodwin admitted in an interview in February that she had failed to adequately attribute dozens of passages in the book." Kirkpatrick, David D. "Historian's Fight for Her Reputation May Be Damaging It." *The New York Times*. 13 March 2002: A18.

5 *The New York Times* published "an accounting of the articles in which falsification, plagiarism, and similar problems were discovered in a review of articles written by Jayson Blair, a reporter for the *The New York Times* who resigned May 1 [2003]." "Witnesses and Documents Unveil Deceptions In a Reporter's Work." *The New York Times*. 11 May 2003: N26.

6 *The New York Times* reported that for one story that was published with only Rick Bragg's byline "interviewing and reporting on the scene were done by a freelance journalist, J. Wes Yoder. The articles should have carried Mr. Yoder's byline with Mr. Bragg's." Steinberg, Jacques. "*Times* Reporter Steps Down Amid Criticism." *The New York Times*. 29 May 2003: A20.

7 According to *The New York Times*, "*Time* magazine and CNN suspended Fareed Zakaria, the writer and television host, on Friday after he apologized for plagiarizing a *New Yorker* article in his column on gun control in the Aug. 20 issue of *Time*." Haughney, Christine. "CNN and *Time* Suspend Journalist After Admission of Plagiarism." *The New York Times*. 10 August 2012: n. pag. Nytimes.com. Web. 7 Nov. 2014.

8 According to *Salon*, "In a case of apparent plagiarism, Fox News pundit Juan Williams lifted—sometimes word for word—from a Center for American Progress report, without ever attributing the information, for a column he wrote last month for the *Hill*

newspaper." Seitz-Wald, Alex. "Juan Williams' Plagiarism Problem." *Salon*. 7 March 2013. Salon.com. Web. 7 Nov. 2014.

9 According to *The New York Times*, "Oprah Winfrey rebuked James Frey, the author of 'A Million Little Pieces,' on her television show yesterday for lying about his past and portraying the book as a truthful account of his life." "Author Is Kicked Out of Oprah Winfrey's Book Club." *The New York Times*. 27 January 2006: n. pag. Nytimes.com. Web. 7 Nov. 2014.

10 *The New York Times* reported, "This week Oprah Winfrey and the New York publishing industry stumbled on yet another unverified account in the form of a Holocaust survivor who said his future wife had helped him stay alive while he was imprisoned as a child in a Nazi concentration camp by throwing apples over the fence to him." Rich, Motoko and Brian Stelter. "As Another Memoir Is Faked, Trust Suffers." *The New York Times*. 30 December 2008: n. pag. Nytimes.com. Web. 7 Nov. 2014.

11 In *Three Cups of Deceit*, John Krakauer wrote, "The first eight chapters of *Three Cups of Tea* are an intricately wrought work of fiction presented as fact." Krakauer, Jon. *Three Cups of Deceit: How Greg Mortenson, Humanitarian Hero, Lost His Way*. New York: Byliner, 2011. ch. 1. Kindle file.

Works cited

Bérubé, Michael. "The Science Wars Redux." *Democracy: A Journal of Ideas*. 19 (2011): n. pag. Web. 29 Jan. 2014.

Bhattacharjee, Yudhijit. "The Mind of a Con Man." *The New York Times*. 28 April 2013: n. pag. Nytimes.com. Web. 29 Jan. 2014.

Brill, Steven. "Bitter Pill." *Time* 4 Mar. 2013: 16–39. Print.

Bok, Sissela. *Lying: Moral Choice in Public and Private Life*. New York: Pantheon, 1978. Print.

Booth, Wayne C. *Modern Dogma and the Rhetoric of Assent*. Notre Dame: U of Notre Dame, 1974. Print.

D'Agata, John, and Jim Fingal. *The Lifespan of a Fact*. New York: W.W. Norton, 2012. Print.

Elbow, Peter. "The Believing Game—Methodological Believing." Paper presented at the Conference on College Composition and Communication, New Orleans, Louisiana, April 2008. Web. 11 Aug. 2014.

Eubanks, Philip and John D. Schaeffer. "A Kind Word for Bullshit: The Problem of Academic Writing." *College Composition and Communication* 59.3 (2008): 372–388.

Gilbert, G. Nigel, and M. J. Mulkay. *Opening Pandora's Box: A Sociological Analysis of Scientists' Discourse*. Cambridge: Cambridge UP, 1984. Print.

Jamieson, Dale. *Reason in a Dark Time: Why the Struggle against Climate Change Failed and What It Means for Our Future*. New York: Oxford UP, 2014. Kindle file.

Kiene, Chelsea. "Joe Barton Cites Great Flood To Disprove Human Role In Climate Change." *The Huffington Post*. 10 Apr. 2013: n. pag. Web. 7 Jan. 2014.

Kinney, David. "Freewheelin': Bob Dylan, Jonah Lehrer and the Truth." *The New York Times*. 2 Aug. 2012: n. pag. Nytimes.com. Web. 29 Jan. 2014.

Kolata, Gina. "Mice Fall Short as Test Subjects for Some of Humans' Deadly Ills." *The New York Times*. 11 Feb. 2013. Nytimes.com. Web. 29 Jan. 2014.

Latour, Bruno, and Steve Woolgar. *Laboratory Life: The Social Construction of Scientific Facts*. Beverly Hills: Sage, 1979. Print.

Lehrer, Jonah. "The Truth Wears Off: Is There Something Wrong with the Scientific Method?" *The New Yorker*. 13 December 2010. Newyorker.com. Web. 29 Jan. 2014.

Lester, Libby. *Media and Environment: Conflict, Politics and the News*. Cambridge: Polity, 2010.

Lovelock, James. *The Revenge of Gaia: Earth's Climate in Crisis and the Fate of Humanity.* New York: Basic, 2006. Kindle file.

Lyotard, Jean-François, Geoffrey Bennington, and Brian Massumi. *The Postmodern Condition: A Report on Knowledge.* Minneapolis: U of Minnesota, 1984. Print.

"Major Trends." *State of the News Media: An Annual Report for 2010.* Pew Research Center. Web. 14 Aug. 2014.

Mann, Michael E. *The Hockey Stick and the Climate Wars: Dispatches from the Front Lines.* New York: Columbia UP, 2012. iBooks file.

Orr, David W. *Down to the Wire: Confronting Climate Collapse.* Oxford: Oxford UP, 2009. Kindle file.

"Retraction." *This American Life.* NPR. 16 March 2012: n. pag. Transcript. Web. 29 January 2014.

Up with Chris Hayes. MSNBC. 10 February 2013. Television.

5 Reasoning backwards is reasoning forwards

Arguments about climate change take place against the general backdrop that I have described. Fair-minded people all agree that what matters most is sound science. But it's difficult to know which scientific claims are sound. Given the broad doubts about truthfulness in the public square, it's no wonder many people hedge their belief in climate science or refuse to believe it at all.

I have mentioned the Pew Research Center's 2014 report that tells us 67 percent of Americans believe that global warming is real. That may seem encouraging, but it really should not be. Sixty-seven percent of Americans do agree that the Earth is warming. However, only 44 percent of Americans say that the warming is caused mainly by human activity. That's a key point. It does little good for people to agree that the Earth is getting warmer if they don't attribute it to human activity. The picture looks even worse when you consider party affiliation: 66 percent of Democrats say that global warming is caused mainly by humans, only 43 percent of Independents, and just 24 percent of Republicans ("Climate Change: Key Data Points").

Climate scientists see things far differently, as you would expect. According to a recent study of peer-reviewed papers on climate, 97 percent of climate scientists believe that the Earth is warming because of human activity (Cook *et al.*). That number is publicized on *SkepticalScience.com*, a pro-consensus website run by the lead author of the study. Of course, we live in a world of constant factual dispute. Climate skeptics argue that the 97 percent figure in Cook's article includes sampling errors, that papers are misclassified, and that their study is methodologically flawed in other ways (Tol).

Nonetheless, I think here is where things stand. There is a strong scientific consensus in favor of anthropogenic climate change (even if it is not precisely 97 percent and even if scientists disagree about many particulars). However, the general public is divided. Many people—in fact, most people—do not fully accept the idea that they are causing it. So there is still an argument to be had. The question I want to address in this chapter is this: What *kind* of argument are we having? How can reasonable people view the same evidence and make such different judgments?

Here is where my analysis turns slightly dystopian. The problem is that people do not simply examine evidence and reach different conclusions. What we are seeing is a competition between two kinds of reasoning. One kind of reasoning is what might be called Enlightenment or classical reasoning: The facts are established, and the conclusions are narrowly and rigorously drawn from those facts. That is how scientists examine questions about the physical world. They may not always reason perfectly, but they always aim to place facts first and conclusions second.

The other kind of reasoning might be called adversarial reasoning—the way most of us make judgments every day. When we reason in that way, we actually begin with a conclusion. We don't consciously reason our way to that conclusion at first; we just know intuitively that it is probably right. And we are correct enough most of the time. Indeed, we could not get through life without making all kinds of assumptions. That doesn't mean we are unreasonable or reject reason as the best way to establish facts. But we only begin consciously reasoning when there is a dispute. At that point, we don't toss our assumptions aside easily. Our default tactic is to search for ways to withstand challenges to our intuitions or to rebut contradictory claims.

What I have described is the "argumentative theory" proposed by Hugo Mercier and Dan Sperber ("Why Do"). They say that this seemingly backwards way of reasoning is not a flaw in the way we think but is, in fact, fundamental to our ordinary reasoning process. If Mercier and Sperber are right, their argumentative theory has profound consequences for public debate. It changes the rules of the game—a game that can have particularly dispiriting contours with respect to climate change.

What classical reasoning sounds like

Climate scientists could hardly provide a better example of classical reasoning. It is evident in their methods and in the way they express their findings and recommendations. I have in mind expositions such as the 2007 *Fourth Assessment Report* from the IPCC (Intergovernmental Panel on Climate Change) (*Climate Change 2007*). The report was written by scientists and approved by a committee, which is not always a recipe for readability. Nonetheless, it is meant to be read by everyone from policy makers to non-specialists.

As a writing teacher, I am inclined to criticize its prose style. To give you the flavor:

> Assessed upper ranges for temperature projections are larger than in the TAR [Third Assessment Report] mainly because the broader range of models now available suggests stronger climate-carbon cycle feedbacks. (*Climate Change 2007* 45)

Even drier:

> Antarctic sea ice extent shows inter-annual variability and localized changes but no statistically significant average multi-decadal trend, consistent with the lack of rise in near-surface atmospheric temperature averages across the continent. (*Climate Change 2007* 33)

There is an acronym for this kind of writing: MEGO (My Eyes Glaze Over). But if the prose style is sometimes obscure, the report is in other respects exemplary. It is meticulously prepared and presents fact after fact. These facts are interpreted cautiously. The report offers abundant qualifications and concessions. It strikes what I would call—as a description, not a compliment—an objective stance.

In fact, it doesn't sound like an argument at all—just a reporting of arid information. I have my doubts that any document can be genuinely objective. I am far more convinced that Bakhtin had it right—that every utterance is a link in the Great Chain of Communication. Thus it's impossible for this document, no matter how steadfast its objective stance, to avoid participating in the public argument. I am also convinced that Stephen Toulmin had it right—that every argument, no matter how reasonable, is guided by underlying assumptions or "warrants." Thus, the IPCC is only credible if you accept its tacit beliefs—such as that statistical models are appropriate and valuable for anticipating future changes in the physical world. From that perspective, the IPCC report simply cannot present reasoning that is fully independent of outside factors or be "objective."

My point is not that the writers of the IPCC report achieve pure objectivity but that they seem to have a benign form of objectivity as their aim. That is demonstrated in many ways, but let me focus here on just one aspect of the report: its intense concern about levels of certainty.

In a 600-word sidebar, the report assigns percentages to ordinary terms to indicate levels of certainty. Here is how they treat likelihood—along with my comments in parentheses:

> "Virtually certain" means the authors are 99% sure of a statement. (Climate scientists are never 100 percent sure of anything. But, then, neither am I.)
>
> "Extremely likely" means they are 95% sure. (This sounds pretty sure. But what does a 4 percent drop represent? A nagging doubt?)
>
> "Very likely" is only 90% sure. (The first drop is 4 percent, the next 5 percent. And then the next drop is a whopping 24 percent. Why isn't "very likely" 75 percent or 78 percent?)
>
> "Likely" is a mere 66%. (To me, 66 percent doesn't sound "likely" at all. It sounds more like "a distinct possibility.")
>
> "More likely than not" is only > 50%. (This is literally correct, but it is perilously close to "probably not.") (*Climate Change* 2007)

There are ten levels of certainty in the scheme, the lowest level being exceptionally unlikely, which is less than 1 percent. Whenever these phrases are used in the report—every single time—they are *italicized*.

All of this may seem excessive. How can anyone tell when they are 66 percent sure of anything? But expressions of relative certainty can matter. In *The Greatest Hoax*, Senator Daniel Inhofe casts a critical eye on revisions of IPCC reports where expressions of [un]certainty were a matter of debate. For example, a draft of the 2001 *Third Assessment Report* said, "*No study to date has positively attributed all or part* [of the observed climate change] *to anthropogenic causes*" (Inhofe 29, emphasis added). The published version says, "*The balance of evidence suggests that there is a* discernible *human influence on global climate*" (Inhofe 29, emphasis added). Inhofe is perturbed by this (to put it mildly) and by similar edits in the 1995 *Second Assessment Report*. He sees them as evidence of a conspiracy among climate scientists to assert their pre-determined conclusions and to silence the voices of dissent. He says that "ideological purity trumped technical and scientific rigor" (159). In fact, the edit sounds like a change in position.

But the lead author of the 2001 *Third Assessment Report*, Michael Mann, explains that the editing process was not focused on general conclusions but rather on how strongly to express scientists' (un)certainty. "Discernible human influence" came about after two days of "haggling" with the Saudi delegate, writes Mann. Originally, the adjective had been "appreciable"; however, the Saudi delegate thought that this was too strong. More than thirty words were considered before all of the parties agreed on "discernible." It may seem a small change, akin to distinguishing between 99 percent certainty and 95 percent certainty. But Mann sees such battles over words as worthwhile. "Why did the scientists care so much about the word?" he writes. "I suppose it comes down to how deeply scientists care about getting things right. Details matter, and we argue with each other passionately about them" (41).

It's worth pointing out, climate scientists can't win with Inhofe. He writes: "One of the most important yet most ignored aspects of the IPCC report is that it is actually quite explicit about the uncertainties surrounding a link between human actions and global warming" (152). For Inhofe, that uncertainty represents a weakness in the case made by the IPCC reports, tantamount to an admission that climate scientists aren't sure of their facts, after all. If they express too much certainty, he accuses them of overreaching. If they reveal their uncertainties, he accuses them of not knowing what they are talking about.

Without a doubt (by which I mean *with 100 percent certainty*), climate scientists are aware of this catch 22—hence the *2007 Assessment Report*'s delicate treatment of phrases such as "very likely" and "more than likely." That linguistic caution is consistent with an objectivist stance, which often means saying precisely how imprecise a finding or prediction may be.

Indeed, the 2007 report emphasizes ranges rather than certain numbers. For example, while it does say that further warming in the twenty-first century is *very likely*, it avoids assigning a precise number to that prediction. Instead, it offers projections based on six possible scenarios, which make different assumptions about population growth, changes in economics and industrial production, variations in natural feedback systems, and so on. Each scenario is assigned a range of possible temperature increases by the end of the twenty-first century. The most optimistic scenario is 1.1–2.9°C; the least optimistic is 2.4–6.4°C. (*Climate Change 2007* 45)

That predictive caution goes hand in hand with the report's full-throated embrace of uncertainty. It closes with a series of "robust" findings, followed by a list of related uncertainties. On the one hand:

> Warming of the climate is unequivocal, as is now evident from observations of increases in global average air and ocean temperatures, widespread melting of snow and ice and rising global average sea level. (72)

On the other hand:

> Climate data coverage remains limited in some regions and there is a notable lack of geographic balance in data and literature on observed changes in natural and managed systems with marked scarcity in developing countries. (72)

And so on.

All of these expressions of uncertainty—a steadfast refusal to be pinned down to specific numbers or to an absolute general prediction (even its strongest qualifier only reaches 99 percent certainty)—would seem to provide a shield against criticism. In Enlightenment fashion, the authors of the report insist on reasoning from evidence and drawing conclusions only to the degree—a rather precise degree—that the evidence supports the conclusions. How can people doubt climate scientists when they doubt themselves so earnestly and publicly?

The way we really reason

Here we reach what may be the point of despair. The science seems so clear; it is presented so even-handedly; its claims are so carefully calibrated—we certainly would be justified in asking once again: Why is there any argument at all? Why do scientists bother with rigorous observation and cautious inferences anyway? If scientists reason to the best of their abilities and others simply refuse to follow where reason leads, what is the use?

The answer to those questions is counterintuitive. And, in ways, it is difficult to accept. Most of us think of reason in the Enlightenment way. We employ reason in order avoid error—to keep from jumping to conclusions. And when we reason that way, we are accountable mainly to our individual mind. That is, we cannot recognize good reasoning except by diligently applying our own intelligence. When we do share our reasoning with others, we expect it to be convincing on its own terms—at least, if it is founded on solid facts, if those facts are interpreted properly, and if our line of reasoning is presented clearly. That is especially so for subjects we take to be purely objective, like physical science.

But when it comes to everyday reasoning, that view may be erroneous—in fact, entirely backwards.

The argumentative theory of reason

I mentioned earlier that another view of reason has emerged in the last decade or two, articulated notably by the cognitive scientists Hugo Mercier and Dan Sperber (also Hélène Landemore) (Mercier and Sperber "Why Do"; Mercier "On the Universality"; Mercier "What Good"; Mercier and Landemore "Reasoning Is For"). They acknowledge, of course, that reason sometimes works according to the classical scheme. It *can* begin with an examination of available evidence and lead to defensible, if not inevitable, conclusions. They say, however, that reason evolved in humans for another purpose: argumentation. They draw an analogy with the human foot. Feet work very well for running, but they are nonetheless better suited for walking. Thus, evolutionary biologists infer that walking is the chief purpose for which feet evolved. Similarly, reasoning can operate in the individualistic, classical way, but we are much better at it when reasoning is part of social interaction—when we argue.

In social interactions, reason tends to work upside down (or backwards or both). We first reach conclusions without being aware that we are doing it. That part of cognition is often called System 1. If we engage in reasoning at all in that initial stage, it is submerged—invisible to us, automatic, and intuitive. Many of our intuitive conclusions are never challenged and, thus, are never subjected to an overt reasoning process. They are just things we know. It's only when they are tested in social interactions that overt reasoning—deliberate weighing of evidence and inferences—is required. So we use conscious, or System 2, reasoning in order to defend our intuitive conclusions and to evaluate counterarguments ("Why Do").

That reversal of order may not seem disturbing by itself. After all, if our reasoning is carefully and honestly undertaken, it wouldn't seem to matter. But it does. When we reason in this upside-down fashion, we do not play fair. That is, when our purpose is to defend pre-existing conclusions, we seek only evidence that supports views we already hold. When our purpose is to debunk others' views, we seek only evidence that undermines them. As Jonathan Haidt, who largely agrees with Mercier and Sperber, puts it, "When faced with a social demand for a verbal justification, one becomes a lawyer trying to build a case, rather than a judge searching for the truth. When we reason about our intuitions, we do not act as detached scientists but rather as lawyers arguing our side of a case" ("Emotional Dog" 814).

In everyday reasoning, we are not required to build a positive case or to have misgivings about our own theories because our aim is to alleviate doubt about our own case and to cast doubt on the prosecution's case. In a courtroom, an adversarial system of argumentation will supposedly bring the truth to light. And that is roughly what Mercier and Sperber suggest happens in everyday argumentation.

They take pains to reassure us that all of this bias is not harmful. They explain that reasoning is a social process. For the most part, we are not the lone reasoners depicted by Descartes. Because we seldom reason alone, our conclusions are always tested. That testing is both productive and beneficial. As individuals, we may be biased in the way we argue. However, as a group, we tend to reach sound conclusions.

In fact, they say that this social process is the reason we have reason. If we were only interested in ensuring that our biases prevail, arguing with each other would have no value. We would be better off refusing to discuss things at all. But, of course, people argue all of the time. When challenged and when challenging others, we require reasoning in order to reassure ourselves that we have reached the right conclusions or that others have not. We have evolved, say Mercier and Sperber, not to reach unfounded conclusions and blindly stick to them but to examine those conclusions when they are challenged—to test them through a process of social reasoning.

It is relevant to observe, nonetheless, that our everyday approach to (un) certainty differs greatly from the approach followed by climate scientists. That difference is problematic for the climate change debate. When we are not bound by scientific discipline, we are so busy defending our intuitions that we are unlikely to vigorously doubt ourselves. Unlike climate scientists writing technical reports, we are *highly unlikely* to concoct schemes of percentages to express just how uncertain we ought to be.

Rebuttal and bias

Mercier and Sperber's argumentative theory is supported by a wide range of experimental research on the ways people reason and argue. In relation to the climate change debate, two related findings seem most important. First, people tend to be poor reasoners on their own, but they are much better reasoners when they are placed in an argumentative situation. For example, Mercier and Sperber cite Deanna Kuhn's 1991 study of people's ability to argue about everyday issues such as the causes of school failure. Kuhn found that unchallenged their participants had great difficulty supporting their views except with banal statements such as that their ideas "make sense." But when put in a defensive position, participants were able to generate reasons for their ideas. In short, when there is no need to come up with good reasons, people leave well enough alone—they satisfice. But when they are put on the spot, they summon the resources to argue their case.

The second important finding is the persistent bias in the way people reason. There is substantial literature in psychology and political science on bias—called variously confirmation bias, disconfirmation bias, motivated reasoning, motivated skepticism, and cognitive dissonance. Contrary to most popular accounts, none of these biases is a matter of simply believing what we want to believe. Instead, they are ways of reconciling beliefs we already hold with contradictory information. It's a balancing act. On the one hand, we want to maintain our beliefs. On the other, we want to be correct. So we have to select and interpret evidence in a way that maintains our intellectual coherence. That doesn't mean our reason leads us to the right conclusions—often it doesn't—but this cognitive balancing is a *kind* of reasoning, not the absence of it.

Mercier and his colleagues point out that such biases are not necessarily harmful. In one study of group deliberation, even when participants initially exhibited bias, the deliberative process bent toward correctness because when people were shown definitively that their conclusions were inferior, they usually change accordingly ("What Good"). But there is an important catch—and it bears strongly on the climate change debate. Deliberation only works out well if the group is intellectually heterogeneous. If the group members are all in agreement to begin with, all bets are off. As Mercier and Sperber put it:

> When all group members agree on a certain view, each of them can find arguments in its favour. These arguments will not be critically examined, let alone refuted, thus providing other group members with additional reasons to hold that view ("Why Do" 62).

It calls to mind the saying familiar to all Americans: "Great minds think alike." Or the similar adage known to Russians: "Fools agree."

The pervasiveness of bias

The climate change debate does not appear to be an open-minded exchange of ideas likely to bend toward the truth. It is acrimonious, polarized, and full of misinformation. So it's important for us to consider whether argumentative bias is the peculiar failing of extreme personalities or something to which we are all subject—casual agreement that makes us ignore contradictory evidence and cling to our beliefs.

When we think of bias as a flaw in our cognitive abilities, it is tempting to also think of it as something found in flawed people. One of the most famous works on biased reasoning is the 1956 book *When Prophecy Fails* by Leon Festinger, Henry Riecken, and Stanley Schachter. Festinger and his colleagues studied a small cult who, like many cults before and after them, believed the end was near. They joined the cult to get an inside look at what would happen when the world failed to explode on the predicted date: December 21, 1954. The group had been receiving messages via automatic writing from the planet Clarion, promising them that a visitor would arrive at midnight, just before the cataclysm, and whisk them off to safety in a spacecraft. However, the visitor did not arrive, and the world remained intact—which might seem reason enough to justify a change of mind.

As it happened, the group did not change its collective mind. A new message conveniently arrived to tell them that the world had been spared because of their devotion. Armed with that confirming fact, their belief grew stronger, and they worked tirelessly to convince others that they had been right all along. Festinger *et al.* call this irrational stubbornness "cognitive dissonance" because the group did not simply deny their error; rather, they found a way to accommodate a dissonant fact into their cognitive scheme.

Such irrational thinking is easy to find among conspiracy theorists. In *Among the Truthers*, Jonathan Kay tells of numerous conspiracy theorists who insist, among other things, that 9/11 was perpetrated by the United States government. Unlike Festinger's cult, these conspiracy theorists do not live outside the mainstream. Yet they hold beliefs that seem, to me anyway, hopelessly far-fetched. Indeed, they work hard and cleverly to prove their theories. Building engineer Richard Gage, for one, gives a 600-slide PowerPoint presentation that demonstrates—fact by fact and photo by photo—that the World Trade Center buildings were not knocked down by hijacked airplanes. The only possible way for reasoning to go so far wrong is for the reasoner to be so committed to a pre-determined conclusion that no fact can disconfirm it.

Of course, the most famous cadre of conspiracists were those who tried to prove that John F. Kennedy was assassinated by multiple shooters, not just by the hapless loser, Lee Harvey Oswald. Not everyone who suspected a conspiracy were con-spiracists. But grassy-knoll theories attracted people who may seem to "the rest of us" to be cognitively aberrant. The original and still the most famous grassy-knoll conspiracist is Mark Lane, who published the best-selling *Rush to Judgment* in 1966 and reiterated his theories as recently as 2011. Lane's indictment of the Warren Commission and intricate speculation about a plot to murder JFK is fact-filled and tantalizing. Lane begins to seem rather an oddball when you learn that, in the course of his career, he became legal counsel for Jim Jones, of Jonestown infamy, and claimed that many of the deaths in Guyana were perpetrated by the CIA.

It is difficult to look at such examples without concluding that there is some-thing fundamentally different about the way "they" think from the way "we" think. But bias is not usually so extravagant. As early as 1990, a substantial body of experimental evidence showed that people persistently select, produce, and evaluate evidence in keeping with their motivations. Ziva Kunda's review of the literature provides many examples of the ways this bias operates. For example, when people want to show that they are academically capable, they selectively recall their academic successes; when they believe someone will join their team in a game, they think highly of that person's skills; and when they receive a good medical diagnosis, they are more likely to believe it than when they receive a bad one. Perhaps these kinds of biases seem commonsensical because they all bear on personal well-being. (For a more recent review of bias, see Friedman.)

But personal advantage is not necessary for confirmation (or disconfirmation) bias to come into play, as we can see with regard to political and moral decisions. In 1979, Charles G. Lord *et al.* published a study of people's resistance to discon-firming information about the death penalty. They asked people to evaluate a series of statements for and against the death penalty: first, a summary statement; then, two papers, one for and one against (both plausible and of equal quality); and finally, a paper that provided mixed evidence. As Lord *et al.* expected, the participants favored the studies that confirmed the view they had already held.

More surprising and more important, the more participants read, the stronger their allegiance to their original view became. In fact, as they read the third paper, which balanced the pro and con evidence, people did not adopt a more balanced view. They scoured it for evidence that supported their opinion. Indeed, a balanced argument did not interfere with people's desires to come up with reasons for their views at all; their biases motivated them to reason even more diligently to justify their belief.

More recently, Taber and Lodge asked people to rate the strength of arguments about affirmative action and gun control. Even though the participants were repeatedly admonished to set aside their feelings, to rate the arguments fairly, and to be as objective as possible, they still rated arguments that supported their view as stronger. They also took more time reading arguments with which they disagreed—all the while formulating their rebuttals. The same kind of bias operates on a larger scale as well. Public opinion polls show that people hold the President accountable for the nation's economic performance during his time in office, but only if the President is from the opposite party (Lebo and Cassino).

Naturally, people have questioned the causes for these biases. It could be that people prefer confirming arguments because they simply think those arguments are more convincing and they prefer Presidents of their own party because they find them to be better equipped to lead the nation. But a key finding in these studies is that people tend to become stronger in their beliefs when faced with contradictory evidence, that they work hard to find evidence that supports their view, and that they do these things even when urged to be neutral. In short, when our beliefs are challenged, we don't just fail to be convinced; we reason defensively.

Bias is also largely unconscious. Studies of moral judgments provide a good illustration. Eric Luis Uhlmann and colleagues conducted an intriguing series of experiments that show how moral judgments can be unconsciously skewed. In one experiment, they asked college students to evaluate different versions of the so-called "trolley car scenario" that were likely to elicit unconsciously biased moral judgments. Some students were asked to read one story, and others were asked to read a similar story that differed in key respects.

In one story, a runaway trolley is carrying a hundred members of the Harlem Jazz Band. The only way to save the band members from certain death is for the moral decision-maker to toss Chip Ellsworth III, who is apparently big enough to stop a trolley, onto the tracks. In the other story, the trolley is carrying members of the New York Philharmonic and the person to be sacrificed is Tyrone Peyton. The racial stereotyping of the names Chip and Tyrone is important here because, as the researchers expected, college students do not want to be seen as racially prejudiced. In both scenarios, the moral decision-maker sacrifices one person to save one hundred others. The moral principle is the same in both cases. But as predicted, the college students rated sacrificing Tyrone as more immoral than sacrificing Chip.

Of course, moral judgments can be tricky. In another experiment, Uhlmann and colleagues asked conservatives and liberals to evaluate the morality of incurring "collateral damage,"—the death of innocent people—in Iraq. In general, conservatives were more comfortable than liberals with incurring collateral damage. They differed in principle. But even allowing for that divergence, there was still a significant difference in the way judgments were made—based on ethnicity. Conservatives were more willing to sacrifice Iraqis than Americans. Liberals, just the opposite.

Given the persistent evidence that people reason in biased ways on a wide range of topics, we should not be terribly surprised that climate change works the same way. A recent study done by Dan Kahan and his colleagues is particularly suggestive in that regard. They compared two ways of predicting people's degree of concern about climate change. One prediction is that the better people understand science and technology, the more likely they are to be worried about climate change. The other prediction is that people's level of concern about climate change is driven by their worldview—Egalitarian Communitarian [that is, liberal] versus the Hierarchical Individualist [that is, conservative].

Their sample was large (1,540 participants) and their results were intriguing. As expected, worldview was a far greater predictor of attitudes toward climate change than scientific and technical literacy. Yet there is an even more disturbing aspect to that divergence. It might be expected that Hierarchical Individualists who understand science and technology well would be at least somewhat more concerned about climate change than those who are less science savvy. However, the opposite is true. Not only were Hierarchical Individualists less concerned about climate change than Egalitarian Communitarians, but also the science-savvy Hierarchical Individualists were the least concerned of all. If you are inclined to discount climate change, a better understanding of scientific and technical matters makes you even surer that you are right.

In short, people's views do not become more flexible as their ability to understand the science increases. What matters is the worldview of the person making the judgment. Conservative individuals, who have a "hierarchical" worldview, are more skeptical of climate scientists than liberals, who have a "communitarian" worldview. Moreover, the greater the conservative's numerical and technical literacy, the greater their skepticism.

Bias and rebuttal in the climate change debate

If people tend to argue as lawyers rather than as detached scientists, we ought to think about how that influences the argumentation surrounding climate change, especially the arguments put forward by skeptics. Skeptics have a different burden of proof than climate scientists, who—like prosecutors—have to present a positive case that can withstand reasonable doubt. Skeptics only have to cast doubt on the scientists' claims. For confirmed skeptics and outright deniers, doubt is easy to come by because their beliefs are so strongly held. In other words, because their beliefs are so strong, they can be confirmed by even weak evidence.

Of course, some skeptics make claims that are better called "disinformation." They spread it with the same insincerity that motivated the tobacco industry when it claimed that smoking does not cause cancer. Indeed, two of the most prominent skeptics, Richard Lindzen and Fred Singer, have had ties to the tobacco industry. So I am not suggesting that we should look naïvely at skeptics' arguments. (For a detailed account of disingenuous scientific debate, see Naomi Oreskes and Erik M. Conway's *Merchants of Doubt*.)

But whatever hard-core skeptics' motives, their arguments are received favorably by many whose motives are not suspect at all. Indeed, if you are already inclined to doubt climate scientists' claims—because you suspect environmentalists are motivated to overstate the case or because you suspect that many scientific claims are likely to be disproven later—skeptics' attacks can be compelling indeed.

Let me provide a brief accounting of the major types of attacks heard from skeptics. I will also point out which ones are more credible than others.

Factual disputes

Skeptics work very hard to discredit climate scientists' findings. In my judgment, these efforts are not especially credible. However, that does not mean the attacks are not persuasive, especially on first reading. Indeed, skeptics often bolster their attacks with impressive-sounding scientific support, and they often raise intriguing scientific questions.

Some attacks rest on a highly dubious estimation of climate scientists' skills and honesty. For instance, Senator Inhofe attacks Michael Mann and colleagues' "hockey stick" graph, which is the line graph that shows a sharp upward turn in global surface temperatures in the twentieth century. Inhofe writes, "Mann's hockey stick completely dismisses both the Medieval Warm Period (800 to 1300) and the Little Ice Age (1300 to 1900), two climate events that are widely recognized in the scientific literature" (ch. 2). Inhofe claims that Mann misrepresents the temperature records because of his scientific incompetence. A portion of the hockey stick data is proxy data from Siberian tree rings, which Inhofe calls "a highly controversial and scientifically flawed approach" (ch. 2). He quotes Dr. Hans Van Storch, "a prominent German researcher with the GKSS for Coastal research" who published contradictory findings in the preeminent journal *Science*: "The hockey stick graph contains assumptions that are not permissible. Methodologically it is wrong: rubbish" (ch. 2). Inhofe also draws support from two statisticians, Steven McIntyre and Ross McKitrick, who claim that Mann's statistical methods are so flawed that even random data will produce Mann's results.

Unless you are well versed in the credentials and positions of those leveling such charges, and especially if the attack is all you are exposed to, the accusation of malfeasance carries a certain force. (I do recommend Michael Mann's account of the Medieval Warming Period, which he and others call not a "period" but an "anomaly," in *The Hockey Stick and the Climate Wars*, ch. 3.)

Also quite powerful are intriguing contradictions. Climate science, it seems, has an endless supply of circumstances that are difficult to explain. Ralph Alexander is a hard-core skeptic who refers to the "so-called consensus" analysis of ice cores and tree rings as "so-called proxy methods," to the IPCC's bibliography as "so-called scientific sources," and to climate scientists' capabilities as "so-called expertise" (ch. 2). He writes, "Although West Antarctica and the small Antarctic Peninsula which points toward Argentina are both warming, the remaining 80% of the continent has shown no significant temperature trend since the 1960s, and may even have cooled up until at least 2000" (ch. 3). This does seem odd. Alexander takes the occasion to attack Michael Mann "of hockey stick infamy" for erroneously insisting on continent-wide warming. He cites the statistician Steven McIntyre, who says that the warming rates are concentrated on the peninsula and are not even half of what climate scientists claim (ch. 3).

Alexander is repeating a standard accusation that had been made and refuted long before Alexander recycled it in 2009 and again in a revised second edition of his book in 2011. Indeed, *RealClimate.com*, which is a website run by mainstream climate scientists, published a thorough rebuttal in 2003, written by Eric Steig and Gavin Schmidt. I will summarize their main points here, not for the sake of the science lesson, but to demonstrate how complex even science written for non-scientists can be. Alexander's task—saying that Mann's calculations are incorrect—is a relatively straightforward rhetorical task. Explaining why that isn't so is difficult.

Steig and Schmidt begin by stipulating that data in Antarctica are hard to come by and that the available data are confusing: the Antarctic Peninsula has warmed; some places in the interior may have cooled somewhat. "At first glance," they say, "this seems to contradict the idea of 'global' warming, but one needs to be careful before jumping to this conclusion." That is because "a rise in the global mean does not imply universal warming." I interpret that to mean that the Earth can grow warmer overall and yet cool off here and there. That is because of "dynamical effects (changes in the winds and ocean circulation)" and "a combination of radiation-related changes (through greenhouse gases, aerosols, ozone and the like)."

Furthermore, they explain, claims that Antarctica is cooling are based on too short a time period, just two decades. A longer sampling—40 years—shows an overall warming. Scientists have too little data to say what the century-long temperature trend has been. Additionally, climate scientists have expected less warming near the South Pole than near the North Pole "due to heat uptake by the Southern Ocean." There is also "some observational evidence that atmospheric dynamical changes may explain the recent cooling over part of Antarctica." In other words, wind has blown warm air away from Antarctica. This wind may have been caused by stratospheric cooling (a result of CO_2 emissions), or it may be a matter of natural variation, which some tree-ring proxy data suggest. Scientists cannot be sure.

May I suggest a small thought experiment? Try to imagine what fair-minded skeptics would make of such factual disputes. How would they go about sorting out what is right from what is not? My surmise is that they might make nothing at all of the details—that they would not be sufficiently motivated to wade through the scientific nitty gritty and note only that there *is* a factual dispute.

Details may not matter in factual disputes, anyway. If you lean toward doubting human-induced climate change, it may be enough to point out that Antarctica is cooling. The data that supports such an attack may not ultimately be credible, but its rhetorical force has little to do with a reader's careful analysis and much to do with which way the reader leans in the first place.

Accusations of corruption

Skeptics' claims of fact are not just a matter of undermining the scientific case for anthropogenic climate change. They also provide evidence for a more damning accusation: that climate scientists and supporters of the consensus view are financially and ideologically corrupt. Again, I find this accusation dubious and self-contradictory.

Skeptics declare full confidence in scientific research that is funded by the fossil fuel industry (an obvious conflict of interest), but say that university scientists cannot be trusted because they need governmental grant money. There are also persistent accusations that Al Gore stands to gain "billions" as he promotes green industries. Skeptics seem much less bothered by T. Boone Pickens' chance for profits in natural gas as he promotes his clean energy alternative. Only those who are deeply suspicious of the government, universities, and Democrats are likely to be swayed by these points of attack.

Yet skeptics won a major public relations coup with what is now called Climategate. In 2009, a cache of climate scientists' e-mails was hacked from the server of the Climate Research Unit of the University of East Anglia. One blogger, Lon Glazner, summarizes the scandal that ensued as follows:

> 1. The scientists colluded in efforts to thwart Freedom of Information Act requests (across continents no less). They reference deleting data, hiding source code from requests, manipulating data to make it more annoying to use, and attempting to deny requests from people recognized as contributors to specific internet sites. Big brother really is watching you. He's just not very good at securing his web site.
> 2. These scientists publicly diminished opposing arguments for lack of being published in peer-reviewed scientific journals. In the background they discussed black-balling journals that did publish opposing views, and preventing opposing views from being published in journals they controlled. They even mention changing the rules midstream in arenas they control to ensure opposing views would not see the light of day. They discuss amongst

themselves which scientists can be trusted and who should be excluded from having data because they may not be "predictable."

3. The scientists expressed concern privately over a lack of increase in global temperatures in the last decade, and the fact that they could not explain this. Publicly they discounted it as simple natural variations. In one instance, data was [apparently] manipulated to hide a decline in temperatures when graphed. Other discussions included ways to discount historic warming trends that inconveniently did not occur during increases in atmospheric CO_2.

4. The emails show examples of top scientists working to create public relations messaging with favorable news outlets. It shows them identifying and cataloging, by name and association, people with opposing views. These people are then disparaged in a coordinated fashion via favorable online communities.

All of this seems quite damning. I have read the e-mails in question, and—to be honest—it is very difficult not to read them in the way this skeptical blogger does. But, the truth is, the e-mails are far less incriminating than they may initially seem. Although the scientists were, indeed, concerned about keeping several papers out of peer-reviewed journals, their concern was prompted by attempts of climate science deniers to publish papers that were not scientifically credible. The scientists were also concerned about discreet handling of data because they had been subjected to onerous freedom of information requests by skeptical groups, the purpose of which was to harass climate scientists and to misconstrue the implications of raw data (Mann ch. 14).

Perhaps the most disturbing part of Climategate was the accusation of data manipulation. In particular, the phrase, "hide the decline," seemed almost indefensible. Nonetheless, here is climate scientist Michael Mann's defense of it:

> While "hide the decline" was poor—and unfortunate—wording on Jones's part, he was simply referring to something Briffa and coauthors had themselves cautioned in their original 1998 publication: that their tree ring density data should not be used to infer temperatures after 1960 because they were compromised by the divergence problem. Jones thus chose not to display the Briffa et al. series, "hiding" data known to be faulty and misleading—again entirely appropriate. (ch. 14)

If I may be permitted a layperson's explanation, the "divergence problem" only means that tree ring proxy data in some time periods does not match temperatures from thermometers. Where the tree-ring data did not seem reliable, the scientists did not use it in the hockey stick graph. It was not a nefarious "trick." As Mann explains, "trick" in this context simply means "clever solution" (ch. 14). The e-mail in question had nothing to do with concealing information that would contradict climate scientists' claims about global warming.

Nonetheless, the Climategate accusations retain significant influence on people's attitudes about global warming. Perhaps that is simply because, as Mark Twain once said, a lie can travel halfway around the world before the truth gets its shoes on. However, it may also be that the accusation of misconduct among climate scientists echoes stories of scientific fraud reported widely in the press and is, therefore, not on its face unbelievable. Couple that with a tendency we all share—to find information especially credible when it supports our intuitions—and it may be easy enough to accept the idea that climate scientists are corrupt.

Accusations of ulterior motives

To believe that climate scientists or public figures like Al Gore are "in it for the money," you have to have a very low estimation of their character. In today's rancorous atmosphere, it does seem possible that conservatives could question the goodness and goodwill of liberals and vice versa. Many conservatives may sincerely believe that liberals and the climate scientists they put their faith in are charlatans bent on foisting a climate crisis on the public in order to line their own pockets. However, that belief may not be as strong an accusation as one that is largely rooted in truth: the accusation that liberals and climate scientists are motivated by loyalty to environmentalism, an ideology that often targets conservatives' lifestyle.

In the next chapter, I will say more about the differences between conservatives' and liberals' worldview. For now, the accusation of *radical* environmentalism is encapsulated well in a response, written by Bonner Cohen, "a senior policy analyst with CFACT," to President Obama's 2013 speech on climate change. Indeed, its title says a great deal: "Obama's Climate Initiative: A Green Elitist Assault on Ordinary Citizens." The response blends charges of an anti-industry tyranny with charges of cultural condescension that are often a part of the climate debate:

> President Obama has—yet again—revealed his determination to subject the American people to the unchecked whims of the federal bureaucracy.
>
> Obama's "Climate Action Plan" has nothing to do with the climate. Instead, the climate, in all of its complexity, serves as a convenient pretext for the administration—working hand in glove with environmental groups and non-competitive, rent-seeking industries—to seize regulatory control of the production and use of energy so as to further concentrate power in Washington. Obama's weapons of choice are executive orders and the regulatory power of the Environmental Protection Agency (EPA), both of which do not require the approval of elected officials in Congress nor those at the state and local level.
>
> Addressing a crowd gathered at Washington's elite Georgetown University (where the annual cost of tuition is north of $44,000 a year), Obama outlined his scheme to rid the world of "carbon pollution." Among

other things, it calls for a 17 percent reduction of greenhouse-gas emissions in the U.S. by 2020, more stringent efficiency standards for home appliances, tougher fuel mileage requirements for heavy-duty trucks, and more subsidies for already heavily subsidized and environmentally destructive (massive bird and bat kills) wind farms.

Much of what is said in this passage is not in dispute. Obama does want to regulate energy production. He does want to and has used executive orders and the EPA. Obama did call for more energy efficiency for home appliances and trucks. He does favor wind power (among other energy sources). The passage really only makes one disputed point.

But it's a big point. Cohen says that Obama's plan has "nothing to do with climate change," that climate change is a mere excuse for a broad environmentalist agenda, and that all of Obama's actions are meant to consolidate power in Washington. More so than factual disputes and more so than accusations of corruption, this accusation reveals the political and ideological tilt of climate change skepticism. If you believe what Bonner Cohen believes, you might find it easy to accept that climate scientists are incompetent and corrupt.

Recoiling from alarmism

From my point of view, perhaps the most worrisome accusation leveled against climate scientists and their supporters is that they both participate in and remain silent in the face of alarmism. That accusation was articulated well in a 2010 Australian television show in which Stephen Schneider, a leading climate scientist, faced an audience of skeptics. One of the audience members says to him:

> What I find suspicious is that I have not heard—and I watch a lot of media— one of these moderately minded scientists come out and hose down the doomsday scenarios being peddled by environmentalists and our politicians. I'm not speaking of you yourself, sir, but your industry—your lobby, the lobby of which you are a part, including a lot of people I'm sure you have arguments with, are actually saying X plus Y all the way to we have to chuck out industrialization. ... I have not heard one [IPCC scientist] stand up and say, "This politician should choose their words more carefully because it's not that disastrous, that this environmentalist should be more moderate in their language because they're being extreme."

In response, Schneider disavows unqualified and extreme language, emphasizing the exquisitely cautious language used by IPCC scientists, which I discussed earlier in this chapter. But remember, it is this same Stephen Schneider who once talked about the need for "scary scenarios" and "dramatic statements" to "capture the public's imagination" (Mann ch. 5).

Schneider might have been referring to what is said on the back cover of Al Gore's *An Inconvenient Truth*, the most famous book on global warming (a companion to the Oscar-winning movie):

> Our climate crisis may at times appear to be happening slowly, but in fact it is happening very quickly—and has become a true planetary emergency. ... In order to face down the danger that is stalking us and move through it, we first have to recognize that we are facing a crisis.

The paperback edition enumerates the threats:

> If we don't recognize that this is a real crisis, the consequences will only get worse. The threat of extinction to endangered species such as polar bears would increase. Water levels could rise so much that millions of people would be permanently flooded out of their homes. More powerful and destructive storms would happen frequently. And that's just the beginning of how the Earth could change forever. (*An Inconvenient Truth*, back cover).

Skeptics may not be right that climate scientists and their allies are alar*mist*s. But they are clearly justified in saying that spokespeople like Al Gore have raised an alarm.

Indeed, concern about overstatement or even alarmism carries some weight for people who are inclined to be moderate and to distrust statements that sound immoderate. Even Stephen Schneider concedes that the worst-case scenarios have only a 10 percent chance of coming to pass. For him, that is threat enough to justify dramatic action. For others, such as the late novelist Michael Crichton, there is far too little to go on. In the appendix to *State of Fear*, he writes, "Nobody knows how much warming will occur in the next century. The computer models vary by 400 percent, de facto proof that nobody knows." Thus, advocates of the consensus view are taken to task for speaking with too much certainty and with too little surefire evidence.

It is worth pausing to reflect on a report sponsored by the World Bank. *Turn Down the Heat: Climate Extremes, Regional Impacts, and the Case for Resilience* warns of a "considerable likelihood of warming reaching 4°C [approximately 7° Fahrenheit] above pre-industrial levels within this century" (8–9). At the 2009 United Nations summit in Copenhagen, 195 nations agreed that 2°C [approximately 3.5° Fahrenheit] is the maximum amount of warming allowable if the world is to avert dangerous climate change. The prospect of doubling the maximum permissible warming is, in fact, alarming.

Works cited

Bakhtin, M. M. "The Problem of Speech Genres." Speech Genres and Other Late Essays. Trans. Vern W. McGee. Austin: U of Texas P, 1986. 60–102. Print.

Climate Change 2007: IPCC Third Assessment Report. "Summary for Policymakers." 7: 33–34. Web. 11 Aug. 2014.

"Climate Change: Key Data Points from Pew Research." Pew Research Center. January 27, 2014. Web. 11 Aug. 2014.

Cohen, Bonner. "Obama's Climate Initiative: A Green Elitist Assault on Ordinary Citizens." *Cfact.org*. 26 June 2013: n. pag. Web. 16 Apr. 2014.

Cook, John, Dana Nuccitelli, Sarah A. Green, Mark Richardson, Bärbel Winkler, Rob Painting, Robert Way, Peter Jacobs, and Andrew Skuce. "Quantifying the Consensus on Anthropogenic Global Warming in the Scientific Literature." *Environmental Research Letters* 8.2 (2013): n. pag. Web. 29 Jan. 2014.

Friedman, Jeffrey. "Motivated Skepticism or Inevitable Conviction? Dogmatism and the Study of Politics." *Critical Review* 24.2 (2012): 131–55. Print.

Glazner, Lon. "Men Behaving Badly." *Commission Impossible*. 21 Nov. 2009: n. pag. Web. 12 July 2014.

Haidt, Jonathan. "The Emotional Dog and Its Rational Tail: A Social Intuitionist Approach to Moral Judgment." *Psychological Review* 108.4 (2001): 814–34. Print.

Inhofe, James M. *The Greatest Hoax: How the Global Warming Conspiracy Threatens Your Future*. Washington, D.C.: WND, 2012. iBooks file.

Kahan, Dan M., Ellen Peters, Maggie Wittlin, Paul Slovic, Lisa Larrimore Ouellette, Donald Braman, and Gregory Mandel. "The Polarizing Impact of Science Literacy and Numeracy on Perceived Climate Change Risks." *Nature Climate Change* 2.10 (2012): 732–35. Print.

Kay, Jonathan. *Among the Truthers: A Journey through America's Growing Conspiracist Underground*. New York: Harper, 2011. Kindle file.

Kuhn, Deanna. *The Skills of Arguments*. Cambridge: Cambridge UP, 1991. Print.

Kunda, Ziva. "The Case for Motivated Reasoning." *Psychological Bulletin* 108.3 (1990): 480–98. Print.

Lebo, Matthew J., and Daniel Cassino. "The Aggregated Consequences of Motivated Reasoning and the Dynamics of Partisan Presidential Approval." *Political Psychology* 28.6 (2007): 719–46. Print.

Lord, Charles G., Lee Ross, and Mark R. Lepper. "Biased Assimilation and Attitude Polarization: The Effects of Prior Theories on Subsequently Considered Evidence." *Journal of Personality and Social Psychology* 37.11 (1979): 2098–109. Print.

Mann, Michael E. *The Hockey Stick and the Climate Wars: Dispatches from the Front Lines*. New York: Columbia UP, 2012. iBooks file.

Mercier, Hugo, and Dan Sperber. "Why Do Humans Reason? Arguments for an Argumentative Theory." *Behavioral and Brain Sciences* 34.2 (2011): 57–74. Print.

Mercier, Hugo. "On the Universality of Argumentative Reasoning." *Journal of Cognition and Culture* 11.1 (2011): 85–113. Print.

Mercier, Hugo. "What Good Is Moral Reasoning?" *Mind & Society* 10.2 (2011): 131–48.

Mercier, Hugo, and Hélène Landemore. "Reasoning Is for Arguing: Understanding the Successes and Failures of Deliberation." *Political Psychology* 33.2 (2012): 243–58. Print.

Oreskes, Naomi, and Erik M. Conway. *Merchants of Doubt: How a Handful of Scientists Obscured the Truth on Issues from Tobacco Smoke to Global Warming*. New York: Bloomsbury, 2010. Kindle file.

Schneider, Stephen. "The Sceptics." *Insight*. 31 May 2011: n. pag. Transcript. Sbs.com.au. Web. 11 Aug. 2014.

Steig, Eric and Gavin Schmidt. "Antarctic Cooling, Global Warming?" *Realclimate.org*. 3 Dec. 2004: n. pag. Web. 31 Mar. 2014.

Taber, Charles S., and Milton Lodge. "Motivated Skepticism in the Evaluation of Political Beliefs." *American Journal of Political Science* 50.3 (2006): 755–69. Print.

Tol, Richard. "The Claim of A 97% Consensus On Global Warming Does Not Stand Up." The Guardian: Environment Blog. n.d., n. pag. Web 2 July 2014.

Toulmin, Stephen. *The Uses of Argument*. Cambridge: UP, 1958. Print.

Turn Down the Heat: Climate Extremes, Regional Impacts, and the Case for Resilience. A Report for the World Bank by the Potsdam Institute for Climate Impact Research and Climate Analytics. Washington, D.C.: 2013.

Uhlmann, Eric Luis, David A. Pizarro, David Tannenbaum, and Peter H. Ditto. "The Motivated Use of Moral Principles." *Judgment and Decision Making* 4.6 (2009): 476–91. Print.

6 Team camo, team khaki

I think it is worth lingering a moment over the first few words of *When Prophecy Fails*:

> A man with conviction is hard to change. Tell him you disagree and he turns away. Show him facts and figures and he questions your sources. Appeal to logic and he fails to see your point.
>
> We have all experienced the futility of trying to change a strong conviction, especially if the convinced person has some investment in his belief. We are familiar with the variety of ingenious defenses with which people protect their convictions, managing to keep them unscathed through the most devastating attacks. (Festinger *et al.* 3)

As I mentioned earlier, the book is about a 1950s cult that persisted in its outré beliefs, even when the world did not end as the cult had loudly predicted. That example may seem a bit far afield from the twenty-first century climate change debate, and I do not wish to suggest that today's climate skeptics suffer from that kind of cultish wackiness.

Yet these two things strike me as relevant about Festinger and his colleagues' observations. First, they draw a seductive analogy between the everyday and the bizarre—the same one we all make. Often when we encounter people who seem impervious to facts and reason, we think of them as a little crazy. That's where we got the term "lunatic fringe," after all. Yet having a strongly held belief, however unusual, is rarely a sign of insanity. And insanely clinging to an odd belief is *not* ordinary stubbornness.

Second, by beginning a book about a cult with the image of one stubborn individual, they suggest a connection between individual conviction and group identity. We often think of failed arguments as one-on-one events—the frustrated arguer addressing "a man with conviction." Even arguments that are broadcast seem to be directed at each individual in the crowd, not really to a collective entity. But Festinger *et al.* are on to something when they equate arguments between individuals with arguments that are infused with group identity. In other words, their "man with conviction" seldom stands alone; people share their convictions with others who reinforce individuals' convictions and sometimes make those convictions more radical in the process.

That is the line of thought I want to pursue in this chapter (and in the next). If we want to make sense of the climate change debate, we cannot ignore people's social and political memberships. It may well be that social and ideological affinities, at least as much as individual reason, drive and derail argument on both sides. Those affinities are what make us say of people who will not see our version of reason: What planet are they from? They must be *insane*.

Climate change on the left and right

Liberals' and conservatives' differing judgments about climate change are plain to see. Consider Governor Chris Christie's response when asked about extreme weather caused by climate change:

> Well, first of all, I don't agree with the premise of your question because *I don't think there's been any proof thus far that [Hurricane] Sandy was caused by climate change.* But I would absolutely expect that that's exactly what WNYC would say, because, you know, *liberal* public radio always has an agenda. (Gonzales, emphasis added)

Christie's statements on climate change have varied. At times, he has been willing to say that man-made climate change is real. But when he needs to appeal to the most conservative of Republicans, he knows which side of the doubting game to play and what term best expresses his exasperation with climate change proponents: "liberal."

Contrast that with President Obama's 2013 speech on climate change, delivered to students at Georgetown University:

> The overwhelming judgment of science—of chemistry and physics and millions of measurements—has put [the scientific debate] to rest. Ninety-seven percent of scientists, including, by the way, some who originally disputed the data, have now put that to rest. They've acknowledged the planet is warming and human activity is contributing to it.
>
> ......
>
>   As a President, as a father, and as an American, I'm here to say we need to act. I refuse to condemn your generation and future generations to a planet that's beyond fixing. (Randall)

Where Christie sees uncertainty, Obama sees overwhelming consensus. Where Christie sees time to consider, Obama sees a duty to act for the sake of "the world that we leave behind not just to you, but to your children and to your grandchildren."

Christie and Obama sound quite different. Yet they can't be entirely a study in contrasts, can they? It seems impossible to me that conservatives would deliberately place their grandchildren in the path of a worldwide cataclysm for the sake of political loyalty or short-term greed. In fact, I've encountered only a few people who respond to the eventual extinction of human civilization with equanimity, and they have been science-minded liberals who view humanity's prospects from a geologic perspective. The vast majority of people, conservatives and liberals alike, care deeply about the future of Earth and the future of humanity. If ever there were an issue to bring liberals and conservatives together, devastating climate change would seem to be it.

Yet liberals and conservatives persistently reach opposite conclusions. Why? The most likely explanation for the divide is that they belong to different social-ideological groups and that these groups reason differently, not only about climate change but also about many other things. Just as liberals are predisposed to be receptive to the findings of climate scientists, conservatives lean in a direction that makes them less receptive.

A similar problem plagued NASA preceding the Challenger disaster. In 1986, the space shuttle Challenger exploded shortly after takeoff. All seven of its crew members were killed, including schoolteacher Christa McAuliffe. The Challenger flight had been imbued with lofty symbolism about reaching new frontiers—about the greatness of a nation. Yet the cause of the tragedy was mundane. Some O-rings failed. To make matters worse, the failure did not come as a complete surprise. Managers at NASA and engineers at their contracted engineering firm, Morton Thiokol, had disagreed sharply about the likelihood of a devastating mechanical glitch.

In the decade following the disaster, a number of rhetorical studies were published about the deliberations at NASA. A particularly striking one was done by Carl Herndl, Barbara Fennell, and Carolyn Miller. Based on analyses of documents and transcripts, they argue that NASA failed to reach the right decision not because of incompetence or carelessness but because two social groups—engineers and managers—evaluated evidence in radically different ways, so different that they simply could not see each other's point.

Herndl *et al.* point out that engineers "reasoned from causes at the level of physical detail—charring and erosion of O-rings. The managers reasoned from results at the level of contracts and programs—successful flights" (302). In other words, engineers relied on data-based predictions that the O-rings would fail. Managers relied on the fact that the O-rings had worked well in previous flights. That is more than just a difference of opinion. Herndl *et al.* conclude that "engineers and managers were unable, more than unwilling, to recognize data which deviated from that characteristic of their organizational roles" (303). The two groups did not even agree—could not agree—on the terms of the argument.

Liberals and conservatives do not have different professional roles, so the analogy with engineers and managers breaks down in that respect. But the differences between the two groups are many, and these differences do lead them to weigh the evidence for human-caused climate change very differently. As I explore this divide a bit further, I want to offer one caution. Some people have argued that conservatives are just deficient—that they reason excessively from fear, that they resist change, and that they have difficulty changing their minds. The left-leaning journalist Chris Mooney writes about the "Republican brain," paying particular attention to science denial. From a slightly different perspective, John Dean (of Watergate notoriety) contends that many conservatives suffer from a personality flaw that he calls "authoritarian mind." A number of psychological studies suggest that liberals and conservatives do not just disagree; they have different cognitive styles. Dan McAdams *et al.* provide a helpful and succinct review of this line of thought.

Studies about conservative thinking are certainly suggestive, and my aim is not to dispute what has been said. But they are often hurled as argument stoppers: Conservatives are not only wrong—there is something wrong with *them!* I want to avoid talking about fundamental cognitive differences in very broad terms. The fact is, we do not need to see a deficiency in all conservatives or all liberals in order to recognize the differences that drive them to disagree about climate change.

Barbara Kingsolver based *Flight Behavior* on those differences. Her Appalachian protagonist, Dellarobia Turnbow, is thrust into the climate change controversy when monarch butterflies, unable to roost in Mexico, descend on Dellarobia's mountain home. Late in the novel, she sizes up the climate change debate for Ovid Byron, the scientist who has come to study the imperiled monarchs. Her explanation has nothing to do with disputes about the scientific method or doubts about this or that fact. It is just that people are different from each other. She tells Ovid:

> I'd say the teams get picked, and then the beliefs get handed around. ... Team camo, we get the right to bear arms and John Deere and the canning jars and tough love and taking care of our own. The other side wears I don't know what, something expensive. They get recycling and population control and lattés and as many second chances as anybody wants. Students e-mailing to tell you they deserve their A's. (498)

The scientist is "stupefied" by her observations. But Dellarobia persists: "I'm just saying. The environment got assigned to the other team. Worries like that are not for people like us. So says my husband" (499).

It may not be entirely accurate to say that we all think what our team thinks, regardless. Even though some of us are relatively independent, we all reason in the context of a polarized argumentative situation. And the poles are magnetized. We cannot help but be pulled toward one end of the debate or the other. As a result, the climate change debate is colored by the motivated reasoning of the contending "sides." Confirmation bias writ large.

How we sort ourselves

The comic novelist Tom Robbins says, "There are two kinds of people in this world: Those who believe there are two kinds of people in this world and those who are smart enough to know better." It's a funny line, and it contains a nugget of wisdom. Yet there is some academic research and serious journalism that support a genuine left-right dichotomy among Americans.

The most startling discussion is Bill Bishop and Robert Cushing's *The Big Sort*. Bishop and Cushing argue that our political polarization is not entirely manufactured by state legislatures that have for a long time drawn oddly shaped congressional districts that lean strongly Democratic or Republican. It is often observed that gerrymandering is so pervasive—and so fine-tuned because of specialized computer programs—that voters no longer choose their elected officials, elected officials choose their voters. However, according to Bishop and Cushing, that's not all that is going on. It's not even our biggest political problem.

Americans are increasingly mobile, and we are drawn to others like ourselves. Over the past few decades, we have sorted ourselves geographically and ideologically. Liberals increasingly live where other liberals live—in large urban areas along the coasts. Conservatives tend to live where other conservatives live—in smaller cities and in rural areas in the South and in the so-called fly-over states in the Midwest and West. Bishop and Cushing demonstrate this phenomenon with complex demographic and electoral data. I will not attempt to do their analysis justice here; however, some simple numbers illustrate the point well.

Bishop and Cushing examine presidential elections by county, which is useful because counties are not redrawn after each census. What they find is a steadily growing geographical partisanship. As of 2008, when *The Big Sort* was published, only a third of Americans lived in a county that had voted consistently for the same party since 1968. But the more recent the cut-off, the higher the percentage. Nearly 50 percent lived in counties that had voted the same way since 1980; 60 percent since 1988; and 73 percent since 1992 (43). To put it another way, the vast majority of Americans live in counties in which the majority has not changed its mind in more than 20 years.

"Majority" is an important word. Not only are counties increasingly partisan in their voting preferences, but they are also increasingly lopsided. In close national elections, you might expect counties to be close too. But they aren't. In 1976, the Carter-Ford presidential squeaker only produced landslides—victories by a margin of 20 percent or more—in 38 percent of the counties. By 2004, when Bush and Kerry kept us all up late, there were landslides in 60 percent of the counties (45). Thus, even in that closest of elections—decided nationally by a margin of less than three percent—a substantial majority of

Americans voted in counties where the outcome was never in doubt. The nation may be evenly divided. But counties are mostly tilted.

That growing partisanship goes hand-in-hand with demographic sorting. As Bishop and Cushing show, compared to Democratic counties, Republican counties are not as highly educated; they are not as rich; they are not as racially and ethnically diverse; and they are more religious (41–57). They sum it up this way: "Opposites don't attract. Psychologists know that people seek others like themselves for marriage and friendship. That the same phenomenon could be taking place between people and communities isn't all that surprising" (41).

The geographical sorting explained by Bishop and Cushing is only part of the story. We don't have to migrate from one physical location to another to seek out preferred news sources in a media, including newspapers, magazines, cable channels, and websites. If we don't want to hear opposing views, we do not have to. Equally important, if we want to hear views that support our own, we can. The question is: Is that what we do?

Communication scholars have studied "selective exposure" since the 1960s, and the results have been mixed. The political scientist Donald Kinder, for one, believes the evidence for selective exposure is "thin." But as communications scholar Natalie Jomini Stroud shows, it appears much stronger when we exclude things like personal care products, cars, and parenting techniques. Politics is a special case. We all tend to select congenial political messages. The stronger our convictions, the more likely we are to seek out confirming voices in print, on television, and on the Internet.

The Internet makes selective exposure especially easy. As many have noticed, people are able to present themselves as they like and view only what they want to view online—to craft what is jokingly called "The Daily Me." But even as we go about pleasing "me," it is wise to remember that we are not one-of-a-kind snowflakes. The legal scholar Cass Sunstein warns that as cyberspace fragments, the result is not individual customization so much as group polarization, a phenomenon in which like-minded people deliberate and then, rather than becoming more reasonable, "move to an extreme point in the direction to which the group's members were originally inclined" (65).

Moreover, the way we are herded into online groups is not just a matter of personal choice. Eli Pariser, a pioneer in online political action, cautions us that even seemingly innocuous Google searches are designed to reinforce what we already know and prefer. That is to say, Google (and Facebook) show you sites and links based on what you have previously searched for and viewed. During the Deepwater Horizon spill, Pariser asked two friends, both of them educated women from the Northeast, to search for British Petroleum. One got news about BP and the spill; the other got investment information. The implications are not hard to imagine. Pariser points out, for example, that a search for "proof of climate change" will yield different Google results depending on one's search history. You might be shown supporting evidence. Someone else might be shown evidence for skepticism.

Pariser sums up the "filter bubble" problem as follows:

> Most viewers of conservative or liberal news sources know that they're going to a station curated to serve a particular political viewpoint. But Google's agenda is opaque. Google doesn't tell you who it thinks you are or why it's showing you the results you're seeing. You don't know if its assumptions about you are right or wrong—and you may not even know it's making assumptions about you in the first place. (8)

What you can be sure of is this: You are not being treated as an individual so much as a kind of person, a collection of data points that place you in a niche with others like you. And the more you are niched, the more you are likely to become like your group.

Moral foundations and conceptual metaphors

Two of the leading thinkers about liberal and conservative ideologies are Jonathan Haidt and George Lakoff. Their work differs in focus and methodology. Haidt is a social psychologist who investigates people's moral and political values. His work draws on ethnographies, evolutionary psychology, experiments, and extensive surveys. Lakoff is a cognitive linguist who examines the way people's political values are revealed in their use of figurative language. His work relies chiefly on linguistic analysis and studies of cognition.

Yet their research is compatible in at least one important way. It shows that liberals and conservatives make judgments about political issues based on values that are deeply entrenched and that operate unconsciously. Moreover, the degree to which their values guide their reasoning is largely invisible to them and to us. As Haidt might put it, we may think that we consciously reason our way to maintain liberal or conservative positions, but we really follow our intuitions about what is right and then we reason our way into maintaining those intuitions. His view is, of course, consistent with the studies I cited in the last chapter about motivated reasoning and confirmation bias.

Jonathan Haidt's six moral foundations

Because intuition plays such a large part in moral reasoning, liberals and conservatives have an extraordinarily difficult time understanding each other, let alone coming to agreements. Haidt explains that there are six core values—which he calls "moral foundations"—that underlie religious, ethical, and political thinking worldwide, as well as in the United States. All of us subscribe to all of these values to a greater or lesser degree. However, the emphasis we place on them differs depending on how liberal or conservative we are.

Since 2008, Haidt and his colleague, Jesse Graham, have surveyed more than 100,000 respondents at YourMorals.org. The survey asks questions that align with moral foundations. For instance, respondents are asked how strongly they agree with this statement: "One of the worst things you can do is to hurt a defenseless animal." If you agree strongly with that, then you place a moral emphasis on the Care/Harm foundation. Similarly, you place a moral emphasis on the Loyalty foundation if you agree strongly with this statement: "It is more important to be a team player than to express oneself."

Liberals score the highest on two of the moral foundations: Care/Harm and Fairness. That is, they care a lot about people who are suffering and who are oppressed. Conservatives share the Care/Harm and Fairness moral foundations, but they score higher on other foundations that do not hold much sway with liberals: Loyalty, Authority, and Sanctity. That is, conservatives do care about people's well-being and about fairness. However, they believe even more strongly that people should be true to their group (for example, to be a loyal American), respect those in positions of authority (for example, the President, the police, and—this is a big one—God), and behave in a clean, pure way (for example, to follow traditional sexual codes).

You may have noticed that there were only five moral foundations mentioned in the previous paragraph, rather than the six that Haidt has identified. That is because when Haidt and Graham first designed their survey, they had identified only five moral foundations. After a few years of research, Haidt came to see a key difference between liberals and conservatives with respect to fairness. Liberals tend to think of fairness as a matter of defending freedom of conscience and freedom from oppression. Haidt now calls this the Liberty foundation. Conservatives think of fairness as a matter of proportionality. They think that people should not take or receive more than they have earned. To take more than your fair proportion is cheating (Haidt *Righteous*).

Haidt is optimistic that once liberals and conservatives come to understand each other's intuitions—each other's moral systems—then we can begin to reason together without the rancor we have observed in recent decades. I can only hope that Haidt's optimism is well founded. But his findings are robust, and they point to significant and consistent differences between liberals' and conservatives' moral intuitions.

George Lakoff and the nation as a family

George Lakoff has conducted a different kind of research but reached very similar conclusions. His most complete statement on liberal and conservative ideologies is found in *Moral Politics: What Conservatives Know That Liberals Don't*. Lakoff's argument grows out of the line of thinking that he and philosopher Mark Johnson introduced in 1979 in their ground-breaking book, *Metaphors We Live By*. Contrary to what many of us learned in school, Lakoff and Johnson argue that a metaphor is not just a device for making our writing more vivid and interesting. You may have been instructed, as I was, not to write, "she is sad," but to enliven your prose with something like "she is drowning in a sea of grief." In other words, use metaphors as rhetorical embellishments.

For Lakoff and a growing number of cognitive linguists, metaphors are not merely linguistic doodads; they constitute the basis of some of our most important concepts. For example, we would hardly know what argument is without the conceptual metaphor Argument Is War. We would hardly know what life is without the metaphor Life Is a Journey. And we would understand romantic love very differently without the metaphor Love Is Madness.

We don't usually encounter these metaphors in short, this-equals-that sentences. Typically, conceptual metaphors are expressed in groupings of standard phrases, complemented with novel variations. We *defend* arguments and *attack* faulty reasoning (Argument Is War). Our lives *take twists and turns*; we *follow the path to prosperity* or *the road to ruin* (Life Is A Journey). We are *crazy in love* or *lose our heads* for someone (Love Is Madness). Some conceptual metaphors apply to particular kinds of activities. For example, I have studied the metaphor Trade Is War (to *conquer* markets, to start a *trade war*) and its complements, such as Markets Are Containers, Trade Is A Journey, and Trade Is Friendship (Eubanks).

As Lakoff has shown, liberals and conservatives alike think by means of conceptual metaphors that embed deeply held ideas about right and wrong, how we ought to run the country, and what its role in the world should be. Liberals and conservatives share the most important metaphor—The Nation As Family—but they construe it very differently. The Nation As Family is an entrenched conceptual metaphor. As George Lakoff explains:

> Our earliest experience with being governed is in our families. Our parents "govern" us: They protect us, tell us what we can and cannot do, make sure we have enough money and supplies, educate us, and have us do our part in running the house.
>
> So it is not at all surprising that many nations are metaphorically seen in terms of families: Mother Russia, Mother India, the Fatherland. In America, we have founding fathers, Daughters of the American Revolution, Uncle Sam, and we send our collective sons and daughters to war. In George Orwell's dystopian novel *1984*, the voice of the totalitarian state was called Big Brother. (*Thinking* ch. 4)
>
> But even if we all use the same metaphor with unconscious ease, it doesn't mean that we make the same use of it. It matters what kind of family.

Conservatives rely on the Strict Father Model. Liberals may shake their heads at this and say, "No surprise there. I already knew that conservatives were all hard-nosed so and so's." In fact, looking at this metaphor explains a great deal and, as Lakoff argues, should cause us to set aside our simplest assumptions about conservative thought. For example, liberals often say that conservatives are driven by greed. But that can't be entirely so because conservatives often oppose policies that would save money and, presumably, lower taxes—policies such as prison reform. Conservatives say *ad nauseam* that they want a smaller government. But they favor an extraordinarily large and expensive military (by world standards). Liberals call conservatives indifferent to human life when they favor the death penalty. But conservatives are quite concerned about human life when it comes to the unborn.

We could throw up our hands and just say that conservatives are full of contradictions or that they're crazy. However, as Lakoff shows, conservative positions seem much more coherent when we take into account the Strict Father Model. It envisions a family in which gender roles are strictly defined. The Father is always responsible for protecting and governing the family. He decides what others should and should not do. At the same time, he expects them to exercise moral responsibility. The Strict Father runs his own family, without the interference of others (certainly without the interference of a village).

When the Strict Father Model shapes the Nation As Family metaphor, it promotes a consistent way of viewing politics and government. In almost all cases, the government should act as a Strict Father would. Why oppose prison reform? Because it is more important to enforce family morality than to save money. The death penalty? The Strict Father enforces moral laws without hesitation or squeamishness. Abortion? The Strict Father is not concerned about preserving his children's right to choose. If they make mistakes (like getting pregnant), he expects them to do the responsible thing. Oppose government regulations? That is a difficult one. We might expect conservatives always to favor strict government rule. But, remember, the Strict Father government has authority over families, which are (or should be) governed by their own Strict Fathers, who have authority not just over the home but also over the family's economic life. From the Strict Father point of view, especially in its U.S. version, it is not right for the government to interfere in family business. (Lakoff *Moral*)

There is a strong similarity between the Strict Father Model described by Lakoff and the conservative moral foundations described by Haidt. Strict fathers are not strongly motivated to protect the oppressed (the Care/Harm foundation). They expect others to measure up—to grow up and take care of themselves. They are not much concerned with children's independent thought (the Liberty foundation). Rather, their job is to protect unchanging principles. As it happens, those unchanging principles have a lot to do with the other moral foundations: Fairness (in the sense of proportionality), Sanctity (correct religious and sexual behavior), Loyalty (to the family and to the family-nation), and—a very important foundation where Strict Fathers are concerned—Authority (which means, of course, respecting and obeying Strict Fathers).

Liberal and conservative metaphors counter each other in diametrical opposition. When liberals think of the national family, they have in mind the Nurturant Parent Model—what conservatives deride as *the nanny state*. Liberals' metaphor emphasizes their dominant moral foundations: Care/Harm and Liberty (that is, freedom from harm and freedom from intellectual, economic, and physical oppression).

Here is how Lakoff *et al.* describe that liberal vision. The Nurturant State's duties include:

- Protection (for people threatened or under duress)
- Fulfillment in life (so others can lead meaningful lives as you would want to)
- Freedom (because to seek fulfillment, you must be free)
- Opportunity (because leading a fulfilling life requires opportunities to explore what is meaningful and fruitful)
- Fairness (because unfairness can stifle freedom and opportunity)
- Equality (because empathy extends to everyone)
- Prosperity (because a certain base amount of material wealth is necessary to lead a fulfilling life and pay for enough shelter, food, and health)
- Community (because nobody makes it alone, and communities are necessary for anyone to lead a fulfilling life) (*Thinking* ch. 4)

These are the values, I would observe, that gave us liberal achievements like Social Security, Medicare, the Civil Rights Act, the Affordable Care Act, and in many states marriage equality. Indeed, the nurturant vision has held steady at least since Franklin Roosevelt articulated the tolerant and caring basis of liberalism in his "four freedoms" inaugural address: freedom of speech, freedom of worship, freedom from want, and freedom from fear.

Are we all on opposing teams?

It is striking to me how both liberals' and conservatives' metaphors make both positive cases and negative ones. Conservatives think that nations and governments ought to behave like strict fathers, and they believe just as strongly that they should not act like nurturing parents. Liberals, just the opposite.

At least, that seems to be so for people who are definitely liberal or definitely conservative. Both Lakoff and Haidt take pains to point out that most of us are not full-fledged members of one team or another (or try not to be, at least). Yet all of us live in a dichotomized world. Our public discourse is self-consciously divided into left and right. It is not subtle. Our political and ideological discourse is clearly labeled.

Indeed, the argumentative situation in which we operate is so stubbornly sorted into liberal and conservative camps that we may not be fully aware of the extent of the influence it has on us. That unawareness is, of course, the root of bias—the ability of our unconscious minds to shape what we think, even when we believe we are fully in control.

Works cited

Bishop, Bill, and Robert G. Cushing. *The Big Sort: Why the Clustering of Like-minded America Is Tearing Us Apart*. Boston: Houghton Mifflin, 2008. Print.

Eubanks, Philip. *A War of Words in the Discourse of Trade: The Rhetorical Constitution of Metaphor*. Carbondale, IL: Southern Illinois UP, 2000. Print.

Festinger, Leon, Henry W. Riecken, and Stanley Schachter. *When Prophecy Fails*. Minneapolis: U of Minnesota, 1956. Print.

Gonzalez, Sarah. "Christie: No Proof Climate Change Caused Sandy." *WNYC.org*. 20 May 2013: n. pag. Web. 17 June 2013.

Haidt, Jonathan. *The Righteous Mind: Why Good People Are Divided by Politics and Religion*. New York: Pantheon, 2012. Kindle file.

Herndl, Carl G., Barbara A. Fennell, and Carolyn R. Miller. "Understanding Failures in Organizational Discourse: The Accident at Three Mile Island and the Shuttle Challenger Disaster." *Textual Dynamics of the Professions*. Ed. Charles Bazerman and James Paradis. Madison: University of Wisconsin Press, 1991. 279–305. Print.

Kinder, Donald R. "Communication and Opinion." *Annual Review of Political Science* 1.1 (1998): 167–97. Print.

Kingsolver, Barbara. *Flight Behavior: A Novel*. New York: Harper, 2012. Kindle file.

Lakoff, George. *Moral Politics: What Conservatives Know That Liberals Don't*. Chicago: U of Chicago Press, 1996. Print.

Lakoff, George, and Mark Johnson. *Metaphors We Live By*. Chicago: U of Chicago Press, 2003. Print.

Lakoff, George. *Don't Think of an Elephant!: Know Your Values and Frame the Debate: The Essential Guide for Progressives*. White River Junction, VT: Chelsea Green, 2004. Print.

McAdams, Dan P., Michelle Albaugh, Emily Farber, Jennifer Daniels, Regina L. Logan, and Brad Olson. "Family Metaphors and Moral Intuitions: How Conservatives and Liberals Narrate Their Lives." *Journal of Personality and Social Psychology* 95.4 (2008): 978–90. Print.

Mooney, Chris. *The Republican Brain: The Science of Why They Deny Science and Reality*. Hoboken, NJ: Wiley, 2012. Kindle file.

Pariser, Eli. *The Filter Bubble: What the Internet Is Hiding from You*. New York: Penguin Press, 2011. Kindle file.

Randall, Tom. "'We Need to Act': Transcript of Obama's Climate Change Speech." *Bloomberg.com*. 25 June 2013: n. pag. 4 Aug. 2014.

Stroud, Natalie Jomini. *Niche News: The Politics of News Choice*. New York: Oxford UP, 2011. Kindle file.

Sunstein, Cass R. *Republic.com*. Princeton, NJ: Princeton UP, 2001. Print.

"YourMorals.Org." YourMorals.Org. N.p., n.d. Web. 2 July 2014.

7   Team camo and team khaki on climate change

Values loom large in the climate change debate, so large that climate activist Bill McKibben writes confidently—and mistakenly: "When we think about global warming at all, the arguments tend to be ideological, theological and economic ("Global"). He certainly knows a great deal about climate change and its disputes. McKibben's website, 350.org, has attracted "thousands of grassroots activists … in over 188 countries." However, arguments about climate change are not explicitly about values. They are, of course, driven by values that are always implied. Yet they are overwhelmingly focused on facts.

When values are explicitly raised, it almost always has to do with accusations of dishonesty and greed. Those who favor the consensus view say that skeptics lie because of their hunger for money. Skeptics say that climate scientists and environmentalists stand to make a lot of money by pushing unnecessary environmental changes. Either that or environmentalists have a perverse desire keep others from making a profit. Sometimes there is a skirmish over religion. Adherents of mainstream climate science accuse skeptics of a religious fanaticism that denies irrefutable scientific discoveries. Skeptics accuse climate scientists and their allies of being blinded by the "religion" of environmentalism. Once these aspersions are cast, the arguments quickly move on to factual disputes.

Bill McKibben can be forgiven for thinking that non-scientific disputes dominate the argumentative situation. These things lie just beneath the surface. Most in the climate change debate, however, make the same assumption that McKibben makes in his *Rolling Stone* article, "Global Terrifying New Math." He begins by saying that too many words are wasted on "ideological, theological, and economic" arguments. Then he turns to what he thinks really matters: the numbers. He plainly realizes that supporters of the consensus view have different values from the skeptics. He thinks that the argument can be settled without reference to such things. In other words, he thinks that facts are value-free, that their implications are plain to see, that they speak for themselves.

Thus it would be fair to summarize McKibben's article in this manner: The rights and wrongs of the climate-change debate are self-evident once you know (1) how much the Earth has warmed, (2) how much we can afford for it to warm, (3) how many gigatons of carbon we can safely put into the atmosphere by mid-century, (4) how quickly we are on track to go past that limit,

(5) how hot things will get if we keep going the way we are going, and (6) how much money the fossil fuel industry (a.k.a. "Public Enemy Number One") stands to lose if we take actions that would put our emissions at a safe level.

The answers: (1) the Earth has warmed about 0.8 degrees Celsius since the beginning of the industrial age; (2) we need to keep the warming at two degrees Celsius or below (that's about three and a half degrees Fahrenheit); (3) to do that, we can place no more than 565 gigatons of carbon into the atmosphere by 2050; (4) the way we are going, we will exceed that limit in 16 years; (5) that means we will get hotter by six degrees Celsius (that's almost 11 degrees Fahrenheit); and (6) the fossil fuel industry stands to lose 20 trillion dollars if we do the right thing ("Global Warming's"). Two and two equals four.

Since most arguments in the climate change debate allow values to lurk in the shallow background, it may be instructive to look at some instances in which motivating values and their attendant metaphors are spelled out for us. These things are sometimes enunciated by the most extreme voices. Yet even that is useful because it shows us what the argumentative poles look like. When we explore voices from the edge, what we find are not oddball metaphors or truly eccentric values, but rather somewhat exaggerated versions of what more moderate people believe.

Voices of the environmentalist left

James Lovelock and Gaia theory

One notable voice from the mainstream of climate science is James Lovelock, a British scientist whose achievements include the invention of the electron capture detector (a device used to identify CFCs [chlorofluorocarbons] in the atmosphere). Although he is admired by mainstream scientists, his manner of expression is far different from the facts-and-figures style of his scientific colleagues.

Lovelock promotes "Gaia Theory," named for the Greek goddess of the Earth, which looks at the planet as a living being whose parts are interconnected and which functions as a large, self-regulating system. Gaia theory is, in part, a scientific heuristic. But it's also a way of valuing the Earth and the creatures that inhabit it. Lovelock writes:

> Only when we think of our planetary home as if it were alive can we see, perhaps for the first time, why farming abrades the living tissue of its skin and why pollution is poisonous to it as well as to us. Increasing levels of carbon dioxide and methane gas in the atmosphere have consequences quite different from those that would occur on a dead planet like Mars. The living Earth's response to what we do will depend not merely on the extent of our land use and pollutions but also on its current state of health. (ch. 1)

The Care/Harm moral foundation suffuses Lovelock's discussion of Gaia. Humans are responsible for nurturing the Earth far more like a Nurturing Parent than a Strict Father. Furthermore, if his language sounds religious to you, you are not wrong. For example: "Those with faith should look again at our Earthly home and see it as a holy place, part of God's creation, but something that we have desecrated" (ch. 1).

In the Gaia metaphor, the underlying metaphoric schema is interconnection. The world is an ecosystem. Human beings are a part of that system. Indeed, the system does not exist for the benefit of human beings, although we do benefit from a healthy environment. We are small in comparison to it. When we affect its well-being, it is usually negatively. The way we stop doing harm to the Earth—and thus restore its healthy interconnections—is to restrain ourselves. Lovelock warns us: "The great party of the twentieth century is coming to an end" (pref.). He also assures us that there is hope for the future, but even then he reminds us that our role has been largely harmful. "Humans are not merely a disease," he writes. "We are, through our intelligence and communication, the nervous system of the planet. … We should be the heart and mind of the planet, not its malady" (pref.).

Many of us might be surprised to hear ourselves likened to a disease or a malady. Conservatives would surely be offended. But we should not write off Lovelock as an extremist or a kook. True, he does upbraid humanity for seemingly uncontroversial activities—like farming. But Lovelock's fundamental values, along with his metaphor of interconnection, are widely shared by others who support the consensus view.

Al Gore

Perhaps more than anyone else, former Vice President Al Gore represents the left-leaning mainstream—not an extremist, no matter how much some on the right insist. Yet his guiding values and metaphors are closely related to those of James Lovelock. In his landmark movie and book about climate change, *An Inconvenient Truth*, Gore concentrates almost entirely on the facts of climate change. At key moments, though, the Care/Harm moral foundation is front and center.

Most strikingly, he asserts the Care/Harm foundation by telling of a personal tragedy—the near death of his son, who was struck by a car and spent many precarious days in the hospital. He calls this a "turning point" in his life. The obvious lessons—to cherish his family and to seize the day in his personal life—are not the only lessons he learns. He writes:

> I truly believe I was handed not just a second chance, but an obligation to pay attention to what matters and to do my part to protect and safeguard, and to do whatever I can at this moment of danger to try to make sure that what is most precious about God's beautiful earth—its livability for us, our children, future generations—doesn't slip from our hands. (*Inconvenient* 71)

The lesson is to value the Care/Harm moral foundation in the global sense.

That lesson requires a particular view of humanity—not to see us as a group of individual actors who pursue our own economic or personal interests but as individuals in an interconnected world, with a responsibility to care for the planet and all of its inhabitants. His call to action reads, in part:

> One way to begin making a difference is to learn how the way we live our lives impacts the global environment. All of us contribute to climate change in the daily choices we make—from the energy we use at home to the cars and other vehicles we drive, from the products and services we consume to the trail of waste we leave behind. (*Inconvenient* 305)

That message is supported by a persistent visual approach. *An Inconvenient Truth*—both the movie and book—displays dozens of images of the Earth seen from space. The planet is presented as an interconnected whole, not as a collection of nations and not as a place for fulfilling individual goals. Indeed, in Gore's telling, it is when we pursue national or individual goals without concern for the planet that trouble begins.

In his earlier book on the environment, *Earth in the Balance*, Gore describes an intricate and intriguing metaphor of interconnectedness. He derives his metaphor from the work of scientists who studied the formation of sand piles. As piles of sand form, Gore explains, they go through stages. At first, each new grain affects only a few other grains in the pile. But at some point—in the mature stage—all of the grains are directly connected with all of the others so that a small change in the position of one grain subtly affects the entire pile. A third stage is possible if a sand pile continues to build beyond its mature stage. The pile then becomes subject to a cascade of changes because the addition of only a few grains can cause traumatic events—avalanches (*Earth*, concl.).

The metaphor operates on many levels for Gore. For example, his son's near-fatal accident was like the addition of sand beyond the mature stage. It prompted a cascade of changes in every aspect of Gore's life. That same logic informs his view of the planet, both physically and culturally. He muses:

> Increasingly, people feel anxious about the accumulation of dramatic changes that portend ever-larger "avalanches" cascading down the slopes of culture and society, uprooting institutions like the family and burying values like those that have always nurtured our concern for the future. The actions of any isolated group now reverberate throughout the entire world, but we seem unable to bridge the chasms that divide us from one another. Is our civilization stuck in conflict between isolated nations, religions, tribes, and political systems—divided by gender and race and language? And now that we have developed the capacity to affect the environment on a global scale, can we also be mature enough to care for the earth as a whole? Or are we still like adolescents with new powers who don't know their own strength and aren't capable of deferring instant gratification? Are we instead on the verge of a

new era of generativity in civilization, one in which we focus on the future of all generations to come? (*Earth* concl.)

Like other framing metaphors in political discourse, Gore's sand-pile metaphor both asserts and refutes. It's not just that he thinks the world operates as an inter-connected whole; It's that he also rejects the notion that we can act as individuals without considering our effects on the entire sand pile. The argumentative force of his metaphor should not be surprising. In the climate change debate and else-where, political and ideological metaphors do not spring forth apart from their argumentative context; they are argumentative through and through.

Sandra Steingraber

More than any other current science writer, Sandra Steingraber places the Care/Harm moral foundation front and center. In *Raising Elijah*, she focuses on the challenges she faces as a mother in a world fraught with human-induced health risks that are exacerbated by climate change. "In a warming world," she writes, "heat waves become longer and more frequent. The higher temperatures speed up chemical reactions between air pollutants—such as car exhaust and evapo-rating paint fumes. As a result, smog thickens, ozone levels rise, and air quality deteriorates." All of this harms children, in particular, by shortening pregnan-cies (a major cause of infant death), by increasing the number of deaths from childhood asthma, and more (ch. 1).

Steingraber provides detailed (though impressively lucid) scientific reasons for her concerns. But the quality of her concerns is at least as striking. In her narrative on motherhood, she faces down a drug dealer over his vicious dog, backing him off of her front porch with the sheer force of her fury. And she describes dramatic episodes of sympathy for the natural world. One afternoon, with infant Elijah napping on a blanket in the backyard, she accidentally runs her push mower over a leopard frog (a species in decline because of chemical pollutants). Steingraber does not shrug off this incident, as many of us might. Rather, "through tears" she sets off to make a donation to an amphibian society in order to "atone for this accident" (ch. 1).

Yet Steingraber's intense protectiveness of her children and nature may not arise simply from personal idiosyncrasy but instead from an especially keen under-standing of the interconnectedness of the world in which we live. She writes extensively about phthalates, which are associated with shortened pregnancies. Phthalates are found in manufactured products from vinyl to hairsprays to per-fume. Thus, it is not one product or another that worries Steingraber; it is the confluence of all of these products. She cites one study, conducted with 331 preg-nant women in New York City. The women carried personal air monitors in their backpacks, and phthalates were found in 100 percent of the air samples analyzed. But it isn't just phthalates that concerns Steingraber; it's phthalates and many other pollutants that conspire to harm pregnant women and, in turn, their babies.

Second-hand tobacco smoke, car exhaust, and smog do their part, too—and all of these are made worse by a warming climate (ch. 1).

Steingraber is a talented crafter of metaphor. In fact, Aristotle might consider her among those who have a "genius" for the rhetorical use of metaphor. Most often, her metaphoric flourishes do not express a worldview so much as they explain a complex scientific process. For instance, she explains brain development as if it were a five-act play. In act two, neurons migrate to form brain structures. She writes, "This migration is highly choreographed. Under the guidance of various helpers, the individual neurons glide along, like dancers in a Russian ballet, to precise locations on the stage" (ch. 8). But in the third act, "Brain development is no longer a ballet. It's an all-night rave" (ch. 8).

But it's not the showy metaphors that tell us the most about her way of seeing the world. Rather, it is the metaphors that seem so apparent that they hardly require an explanation. Consider Steingraber's dispute over play structures at her son Elijah's preschool.

The play structures were constructed of pressure-treated lumber that contained arsenic—a carcinogen whose effects take 20 to 45 years to appear. Several parents, including Steingraber, wanted the preschool to remove the play structures (mainly because children touch things and then put their hands into their mouths). A lab test of the play structures showed that they did expose children to significant levels of arsenic. But as Steingraber observes, "The arsenic data ... were numbers onto which an individual could project a worldview" (ch. 2). Some parents saw the risks as minimal and argued the case with their own analysis of the numbers. Unsurprisingly, their "equations and spreadsheets" showed that "health risks from playground-derived arsenic were minimal" (ch. 2).

Thus, the play structures dispute functions as a revealing metaphor for the worldviews that shape the climate change debate. From Steingraber's perspective, the arsenic-infused play structures present yet another example of the way apparently small causes can have large effects. It speaks broadly about careless attitudes toward our environment(s). For others, it is another example of alarmism. The play structure dispute is a microcosm, not different in kind from the debate about climate change.

Indeed, for Steingraber, the parallel is clear. She notes the discontinuity we experience:

> [W]hen we are told that a problem is dire (mass extinctions, melting ice caps) but the proposed solution (buy new light bulbs) seems trivial. If the problem were really so dire, wouldn't we all be asked to respond with action of equivalent magnitude? (ch. 2)

By the same token, "If pressure-treated playgrounds were really so dangerous—I could imagine parents thinking—wouldn't the EPA or the Product Safety Commission have demanded an immediate recall?" (ch. 2).

David Orr

Climate change skeptics and deniers are fond of calling people in the consensus "alarmists." David Orr fills that bill quite well. Indeed, I have no doubt that he would embrace the title on the grounds that climate change—he prefers the term "climate disruption"—is upon us, and we ought to be alarmed. In his view, this "long emergency" has been brought about not by the happenstance inventions of the industrial age but rather as the sad result of individuals' and capitalism's excesses that desperately need to be replaced by new collective efforts. His vision calls to mind socialism so readily that he takes pains to deny it: "My position is not 'socialist,' whatever that word is presumed to mean, but it is decidedly in favor of placing limits on corporate power and even individualism where its excesses cast long shadows on the prospects of our grandchildren and theirs" (39).

If Orr has any kind of "socialist" agenda, it is not of the sort that includes five-year plans and May Day parades. Rather, he has in mind—in the same way that Lovelock and Gore have in mind—an interconnected planet, a planetary system in which humans play a role in the larger scheme and only imagine their individuality is real. He draws support for that view from Albert Einstein, who wrote, "a human being is part of the whole world, called by us 'Universe,' a part limited in time and space. He experiences himself, his thoughts and feelings as something separate from the rest—a kind of optical delusion of his consciousness." (Quoted in Orr 76)

For Orr, humanity's responsibilities to the Universe are quite specific; or, at least, humanity's transgressions against it are. His list of complaints and desires would ring true, I believe, to most liberals:

> The fact is that climate stability, sustainability, and security are impossible in a world with too much violence, too many weapons, too much unaccountable power, too much stuff for some and too little for others, and a political system that is bought and paid for behind closed doors. Looming climate catastrophe, in other words, is a symptom of a larger disease. (189)

Indeed, like James Lovelock, Orr sees the world—its physical being and its culture—as an organism that is sick because of the things we do. "What do I propose?" he writes,

> Simply this: that those who purport to lead us, and all of us who are concerned about climate change, environmental quality, and equity, treat the public as intelligent adults who are capable of understanding the truth and acting creatively and courageously in the face of necessity—much as a doctor talking to a patient with a potentially terminal disease. (189)

Of course, his view of climate change is guided almost solely by the Care/Harm moral foundation, which means that addressing climate change is a moral responsibility. "It is up to us," he says, "to be active citizens again, to know more, think more deeply, take responsibility, participate publicly, and, from time to time, to sacrifice" (190).

If Orr calls on us to sacrifice now, it is only so that we can create a sort of utopia in the future. He is specific about that utopia, too—a world custom made, it seems, for enlightened people in the liberal enclaves of the United States. And, conversely, a world certain to repel conservatives, who might find it alarming, but would unquestionably find it odd. Orr provides us with a convenient list of what an idyllic carbon-free future might include. I have inserted in brackets what I suspect would be the (ultra)conservative response.

Front porches
[Liberals hate all-American things like big yards and backyard decks.]

Public parks
[Liberals love it when the government seizes land and imposes a lot of rules about how we can use it.]

Local businesses
[Liberals hate corporations.]

Windmills and solar collectors
[Liberals hate oil, nuclear, and coal.]

Living machines to process waste water
[Liberals would love to put these things right next to their compost piles.]

Local farms and better food
[Liberals hate corporate farming.]

More and better woodlots and forests
[Liberals love things that create more government land and more government control.]

Summer jobs for kids doing useful things
[Liberals always define useful as personally fulfilling, not profitable.]

Local employment
[Liberals can't resist a swipe at corporations.]

More bike trails
[Liberals love bike trails and hate the roads we need for real vehicles like cars, trucks, and SUVs.]

Summer baseball leagues.
[Liberals hate football.]

Community theaters
[Liberals hate football.]

Better poetry
[Poetry is for artsy liberals.]

Neighborhood book discussion groups
[They'll be full of artsy, preachy liberals.]

Bowling leagues
[Bowling is good.]

Better schools
[Liberals want to produce intellectuals interested in the humanities, not the STEM students needed by industry.]

Vibrant and robust downtowns with sidewalk cafés
[Liberals hate malls and Walmart—and love all things French.]

Great pubs serving microbrews
[Liberals can't resist a swipe at corporations.]

Fewer freeways, shopping malls, sprawl, and television
[We'll all be bicycling to the French sidewalk café to read liberal poetry.]

More kids playing outdoors
[But liberals won't let them play football.]

No more wars for oil or access to other people's resources
[Naturally, liberals refuse to protect America from its enemies.] (190)

Orr's list is easy to lampoon, I suppose—so easy that you might suspect me of choosing an obscure nugget for that very purpose. But I am not the only one attracted by this passage. The Center for Ecoliteracy—"a nonprofit that advances ecological education in K–12 schools [so students can] experience and understand how nature sustains life and how to live accordingly"—uses the very same excerpts on its climate change webpage ("On Climate Change"). As someone who leans more left than right, I must confess that nearly everything Orr envisions sounds wonderful to me, except for better poetry. I doubt poets will find love more urgent or life more poignant if we just get control of our carbon emissions.

Lovelock, Gore, Steingraber, and Orr on the purity of the Earth

Jonathan Haidt found that conservatives, far more than liberals, rely on sanctity or purity as a moral foundation. He also points out that liberals sometimes have their own version of sanctity or purity. In recent years, that is evident in the way people on the left think about food. Enter any co-op grocery and you will see organically grown food, free of preservatives, often locally produced, and brought to market via fair trade practices. Many on the left promote these qualities with a quasi-religious conviction, which goes hand in hand with a strong disapproval of companies that profit from foods that are unhealthy or impure.

In the environmental movement and in the discourse of climate change, that same emphasis on natural purity applies to the entire Earth. Consider the implications of David Orr's Jeffersonian language about our duties to the Earth:

> No generation and no nation has the right to alter the biogeochemical cycles of Earth or impair the stability, integrity, or beauty of natural systems, the consequences of which would fall as a form of intergenerational remote tyranny on all future generations. (76)

Or consider the religious intonation of James Lovelock's Gaia, which he says is a concept that can only be known intuitively, like God—"ineffable," "immanent but unknowable." He muses that perhaps Christians need "a new Sermon on the Mount that sets out the human constraints needed for living decently with the Earth" and wishes that both the religious and secular humanists would "turn to the concept of Gaia and recognize that human rights and needs are not enough" and "accept the Earth as part of God's creation and be troubled by its desecration" (ch. 8).

Or consider Sandra Steingraber's pointed simile, "Fossil fuels are like cigarettes for the planet" (ch. 6).

Or consider the movie trailer for *An Inconvenient Truth*, in which Al Gore pronounces, "This is really not a political issue so much as a moral issue." In which we see flashed across the screen in capital letters: DID THE PLANET BETRAY US ... OR DID WE BETRAY THE PLANET? ("An Inconvenient") And which closes with a satellite photograph of the Earth floating in space.

The voices of the free-market right

Defenders of the marketplace

Liberals often believe that conservatives are driven by greed. Truth be told, conservatives do a very good job of reinforcing that stereotype. Skeptics' arguments usually concentrate on challenging climatolgists' findings—relentlessly so. Sooner or later, though, they raise the question of profits. Consider, for example, a *Wall Street Journal* (*WSJ*) editorial that probes weaknesses in the fifth IPCC report. It says,

> Though the IPCC doesn't admit it, the real lesson of its report is uncertainty. Droughts and hurricanes? Contrary to Al Gore's hype, the report acknowledges there's little evidence to suggest that climate change caused by man has had much to do with the duration of droughts or the intensity of hurricanes, although it might in the far future.
>
> Unbearable heat? The IPCC predicts that temperatures are "likely" to rise by somewhat more than 1.5 degrees Celsius throughout the rest of the century. But in 2007 the IPCC said they were "likely" to increase by more than 2 degrees, and "very unlikely" to increase by less than 1.5 degrees. ("Climate of Uncertainty")

Indeed, the *WSJ* pounces on any change from the fourth IPCC report, as if it were not a normal part of the scientific process for new information to lead to revised judgments. It observes, "It's also hard to take any of this as gospel when the IPCC's climate models haven't been able to predict past warming" ("Climate of Uncertainty").

There is a "tell" in this editorial, liberals might say. At the end of the piece, the focus turns to economic disputes. The *WSJ* accuses the IPCC of using

> flimsy intellectual scaffolding ... to justify killing the U.S. coal industry and the Keystone XL pipeline, banning natural gas drilling, imposing costly efficiency requirements for automobiles, light bulbs, washing machines and refrigerators, and using scarce resources to subsidize technologies that even after decades can't compete on their own in the marketplace. ("Climate of Uncertainty")

So it's really about money. At least, that's what the *WSJ* says about the IPCC, whose aim is to give "more economic control to political actors whose interventions make the world poorer than it would otherwise be" ("Climate of Uncertainty").

Other skeptical voices blend factual disputations with economic concerns in much the same way. The Heartland Institute, for instance. Climate activists Dan Becker and James Gerstenzang identify the Heartland Institute as one of the "think tanks and front groups funded by oil, coal and others with a financial stake in the debate." Heartland would, of course, say that their funding or financial interests do not influence their position on climate science. At the same time, they make no secret of their mission, which is "to discover, develop, and promote free-market solutions to social and economic problems" and which, of course, redounds to the benefit of their financers.

Yet the skeptics' focus on money may not be as simple as pure greed, even if the so-called denial machine is funded by fossil fuel industries. True, the denial machine is akin to—and in some cases directly linked to—the disinformation machine that defended the tobacco industry in recent decades. But that kind of venality cannot explain a broader conservative emphasis on immediate economic concerns. Even Judith Curry, a mainstream scientist who is sympathetic to skeptics' uncertainty about climate change, remarks about her nieces' and nephews' economic interests: "Are we going to jeopardize their economic future, and we don't know if they're going to care and if this is going to matter?" (Harris).

As I discussed in the last chapter, a more likely explanation for conservatives' emphasis on immediate economic worries can be found in the values and metaphors that shape conservative thought. As Lakoff explains, the Strict Father Model requires economic non-interference from the government. That is, the government is expected to honor the independence of families and the strict fathers who lead them (*Moral*). Furthermore, as Jonathan Haidt has shown, conservatives rely on moral foundations that liberals care very little about (*Righteous*). Two of them are fairness (in the sense of proportionality—earn what you keep, keep what you earn) and loyalty (to their social groups and to the nation).

All of these things—a dislike of government interference, a belief in proportionality, and national loyalty—underpin skeptics' arguments about climate change. Consider the way Fred S. Singer and Dennis Avery warn us against an extension of the Kyoto Protocol:

> A new climate change treaty would at least pay lip service to the obligations of developing nations, though it could probably not require them to reduce emissions. Instead, the new Kyoto might be shaped by the notion of "contraction and convergence," now popular in European environmental circles.
>
> The concept is that every human being on this planet has the right to emit the same amount of carbon dioxide. Therefore, citizens of developing nations would be given the same quota for emissions as citizens in industrialized nations. The latter would have the privilege of buying unused emission rights from those who are not using their allocated quota. In other words, the world would see a giant cash transfer from developed to developing nations. (230–31)

It is possible to see greed in their argument. But if it is greed, it is greed founded on standard conservative values that resonate with people who have little to gain directly from the success of fossil fuels, except to maintain the kind of lifestyle they have worked to achieve.

To conservatives, it does not seem right for governments, either in the form of the United Nations or as signatories to the Kyoto protocol, to make us all "emit the same amount of carbon dioxide" because it is not proportional to what each of us has earned. The treaty would only "pay lip service" to making developing countries do their fair share and it would give them money that is not rightly theirs—"a giant cash transfer from developed to developing nations."

Non-proportionality is not the only problem with Kyoto-like agreements. They amount to a government assault business and the economic lives of families. Singer and Avery write,

> Imagine an America in which you are allowed to drive your auto only two days per month; in which air conditioning is banned from homes and offices; in which the Iceman cometh daily, because there are no electric refrigerators. Imagine the sun belt being evacuated. How much industrial and business investment would become useless? (232)

Perhaps, Singer and Avery would be willing to submit to all of these things if they believed global warming were a genuine threat. However, their fear is not just that governments will force non-proportional and disloyal policies on Americans, but also that coercion, not environmental prudence, is environmentalists' hidden goal.

Brian Sussman

Brian Sussman is a former television meteorologist, a current conservative radio personality, and a strident objector to environmentalism and communism—which he believes are, more or less, the same thing. Even among skeptics and deniers, he stands out for his scathing attacks on environmentalists, especially mainstream climate scientists. Here is what he says about environmentalists in *Eco-Tyranny: How the Left's Green Agenda Will Dismantle America*:

> Environmentalist activists are dogmatic, ideological radicals hell-bent on transforming society into a colossal, highly regulated, redistributive commune void of inalienable rights. Their lack of integrity enables them to look you straight in the eye and lie about the facts, as they spin out tailor-made, cherry-picked research supposedly proving their many fictitious claims regarding the state of the global ecosystem. (ch. 2)

It is fair to say, I believe, that Sussman does not concern himself with rhetorical restraint. Yet his underlying values are not odd; they are ordinary conservative values, leavened with heightened paranoia.

What drives Sussman's outsized fears is not so much a metaphor as a metonymy, the figure of contiguity. Where people in the consensus see an interconnected universe that can be likened to an ecosystem out of balance or an ailing human body or an unstable pile of sand, Sussman sees a series of links that lead from the land to the individual. As he explains, "The term 'property,' as understood by America's founders, … includes one's thoughts, opinions, beliefs, ideas, and unalienable rights" (forew.). That capacious definition of property defines his understanding of the Earth, which is, for him, properly parceled out as bits of private property. When the government seizes control of a citizen's land, it takes more than dirt and buildings; it steals the basis for that person's thoughts, opinions, beliefs, ideas, and unalienable rights. The seizing of one kind of property is tantamount to seizing all kinds of property.

Because of that, Sussman is fixated on government lands—700 million acres of it—including national parks, which are controlled by "guntoting agencies" such as the Forest Service and the Department of the Interior. This is just the beginning. President Obama, he tells us, has a secret plan "to purchase, or take over, millions of acres of private property in order to connect land owned by, and managed by, the federal government." The ultimate goal of Obama's secret plan is to "divide the country into sectors where all humans would be herded into urban hubs with the bulk of the nation's land returned to a natural state upon which humans will only be allowed to tread lightly" (forew.).

At the end of *Eco-Tyranny*, Sussman asks us to imagine the world of 2050 if the environmentalists are allowed to take over. The United States is no longer made up of states but of megaregions. Americans are forced to live in urban hubs in small apartments. People under the environmentalists' thumbs now brag about how small their living space is because it follows the new maxim: "Keep thy footprint small and, thus, [be] a good citizen of the planet." Transportation has been taken over by high-speed rail, electric cars, bicycles, and walking. The only cars to be found are "subcompact pretend-cars." Patriotism has been so transformed that it is unrecognizable. The American flag is now red, white, and green. There is a national anthem, but it's now the peaceful tribute to nature, "America the Beautiful." It is sung at the start of professional *soccer games*. As for the green spaces, they have been cordoned off as vast "wildways," devoid of private ranches, farms, and small towns. People are only allowed to speed through them on electric trains, from urban hub to urban hub (ch. 12).

It sounds a bit far-fetched. Yet is it so different from the utopia imagined by David Orr—with its woodlands and forests, vibrant downtowns filled with sidewalk cafés, bicycle trails, book clubs, and better poetry? Whatever it is—paranoid vision or lampoon of liberals' dreams—it is founded on two familiar moral foundations, ones that are shared by tens of thousands of the self-identified conservatives surveyed by Jonathan Haidt. Sussman fears the loss of national identity—the group to which he is loyal. He objects to unfairness because in this dystopian future, people cannot buy goods in proportion to what they have earned—no cars, no ranches, no big houses. Lurking in the background, as always, is the Strict Father Model of the Nation As Family, with its distaste for government nurturing and government interference in people's economic lives.

Senator James Inhofe

Brian Sussman is a character from the fringe. But it is difficult to say that about U.S. Senator James Inhofe. Like Al Gore, he represents his party's mainstream—a party that, many have observed, has become radicalized. In fact, his point of view is much like that of Sussman. He doubts environmentalists' intentions, worries about economic growth, and sees a strong link—a metonymy—between land and property and the rights of individuals.

His anti-consensus book, *The Greatest Hoax*, begins with this statement from Czech President Vaclav Klaus:

> The global warming religion is an aggressive attempt to use the climate for suppressing freedom and diminishing our prosperity. Senator Inhofe's book is an important contribution in the fight against this totally erroneous doctrine which has no solid relation to the science of climatology but is about power in the hands of unelected global warming activists. (endorsements)

Inhofe argues, using example after example, that our freedom is suppressed through regulation of all kinds of property—land, buildings, the right to use carbon, everything. President Obama, he says, wants to regulate virtually every aspect of American life "from farm dust to puddles of water on the road" (intro.). It's all part of environmentalists' desire to curtail a way of life that he and the people he cares about value. He complains that a hypocritical Hollywood elite demands that "Americans use only one square of toilet paper, take cold showers or two-minute showers, not eat meat, and take public transportation, while clearly they were not willing to make sacrifices themselves" (ch. 4).

That metonymy—property rights contiguous with a way of life—extends to carbon. He writes (and quotes the prominent scientist-skeptic Richard Lindzen):

> Looking back, it is clear that the global warming debate was never really about saving the world; it was about controlling the lives of every American. MIT climate scientist Richard Lindzen summed it up perfectly in March 2007 when he said, "Controlling carbon is a bureaucrat's dream. If you control carbon, you control life." (ch. 1)

It is hard to imagine a greater regulatory overreach than controlling life. But that is exactly what Inhofe fears and suspects is going on. His fear is based on a series of metonymies that link small government actions to large injustices.

Consider Inhofe's fire escape example. Just as Al Gore credits his son's near-fatal accident with motivating him to save the world (literally), Inhofe says that his involvement in politics and his current campaign to debunk mainstream climate science began with a dispute with Tulsa's city engineer. In a chapter titled "Why I Fight," he tells of the time he purchased an old building and planned to move a fire escape from the front of the building to the back (where it would not be an eyesore). The city engineer, however, was not receptive and told Inhofe he would have to take up the matter with the city county—in 2 months.

Here is Inhofe's account of their uncomfortable conversation:

> "Two months?" I exclaimed, "This project can't be delayed that long because all the workers are being paid now. That will cost me thousands of dollars. Are you telling me you won't help me at all?" He just looked at me and said, "That's your problem, not mine." So I told him that I was going to run for Mayor and fire him. And I ran for mayor and I fired him. (ch. 1)

It may seem quite a leap from a dispute about a local building code to a scientific dispute that may involve the fate of civilization. But in Inhofe's view, the connection is plain to see.

Metaphoric chickens and metonymic eggs

It is difficult to know, I admit, whether climate skeptics and deniers justify their greed by appealing to bedrock conservative values or whether those bedrock values lead them to champion causes—like energy from coal and oil—that are easily mistaken for greed. I suspect that the two things are so intertwined that they could never be disentangled. The same is certainly true for people in the consensus, which is associated mainly with liberalism. Is it possible to care about the future of the Earth and future civilization without placing a high priority on the Care/Harm moral foundation? Liberals have not always been advocates for science, especially when it has been associated with military weaponry. But when science aligns with saving people from harm and, in particular, preventing unfair oppression of disadvantaged people (a predicted consequence of climate change), then science and moral values seem inevitably bound together.

Works cited

350.org. "About." Web. 27 Apr. 2014.

"An Inconvenient Truth Created by Al Gore." *An Inconvenient Truth RSS*. N.p., n.d. Web. 2 July 2014.

Becker, Dan and James Gerstenzang. "Climate Deniers, Meet Joe Camel." *Huffington Post*. 29 Oct. 2013. n. pag. Web. 6 Jan. 2014.

"Climate of Uncertainty: A U.N. Report Can't Explain the Hiatus in Global Warming." *Wall Street Journal*. 1 Oct. 2013: n. pag. Web. 11 Aug. 2014.

Gore, Albert. *An Inconvenient Truth*. New York: Viking, 2007. Print.

——*Earth in the Balance: Ecology and the Human Spirit*. Boston: Houghton Mifflin, 1992. Kindle file.

Haidt, Jonathan. *The Righteous Mind: Why Good People Are Divided by Politics and Religion*. New York: Pantheon, 2012. Kindle file.

Harris, Richard. "Uncertain' Science: Judith Curry's Take on Climate Change." *NPR.org*. 22 Aug. 2013: n. pag. Web. 19 Mar. 2014.

Lakoff, George. *Moral Politics: What Conservatives Know That Liberals Don't*. Chicago: U of Chicago Press, 1996. Print.

Lovelock, James. *The Revenge of Gaia: Earth's Climate in Crisis and the Fate of Humanity*. New York: Basic, 2006. Kindle file.

McKibben, Bill. "Global Warming's Terrifying New Math." *Rolling Stone*. 19 July 2012: n. pag. Rollingstone.com. Web. 28 Apr. 2014.

"On Climate Change and Applied Hope." *Ecoliteracy.com*. n. pag. Web. 15 Apr. 2014.

Orr, David W. *Down to the Wire: Confronting Climate Collapse*. Oxford: Oxford UP, 2009. Kindle file.

Singer, Siegfried Fred, and Dennis T. Avery. *Unstoppable Global Warming: Every 1500 Years*. Lanham, MD: Rowman & Littlefield, 2008. Kindle file.

Steingraber, Sandra. *Raising Elijah: Protecting Our Children in an Age of Environmental Crisis*. Cambridge, MA: Da Capo, 2011. Print.

Sussman, Brian. *Eco-Tyranny: How the Left's Green Agenda Will Dismantle America*. Washington, D.C.: WND Books, 2012. Kindle file.

8   The attention imperative

In his classic treatise on argumentation, Stephen Toulmin pointed out that an argument's central claim has two aspects. It is a claim that something is true. It is also a claim on an audience's attention (11). To put it another way, a good argumentative claim has to do more than tell you something that is well supported by evidence and reason; it has to be worth a piece of your finite mental resources. We live in an atmosphere in which everyone and everything vies for our attention, including what would seem to be, by their very nature, rather dry arguments. I want to call this persistent and omnipresent effort to stake a claim on our time and interest the *attention imperative*.

It is part and parcel of what Richard Lanham has termed "the economics of attention." Lanham points out that in the so-called information age, the discursive economy is shaped very little by the need for information itself. That commodity is not in short supply, far from it. But an ocean of information is of no use to us unless someone calls our attention to a relevant portion of it and presents it in a way that helps us to make sense of it. As Lanham reminds us, the study of rhetoric has always been concerned with how the substance of things can be joined most effectively with style—how a speaker (and later a writer) can most effectively direct the attention of an audience.

If we have long thought about the need to get an audience's attention, we have not always faced the types of challenges we confront in the digital age. The amount of information available to us has grown hand-in-hand with the chance for all of us to speak. Lanham sees this as a largely positive development and admires the willingness of countless people to mount the world stage in order to share information about anything and everything. A case in point: When I first began collecting climate change material, Amazon displayed on an equal footing with books by Senator James Inhofe and Professor Michael Mann an e-book by Joseph Patrick Noonan, who calls himself "a typical middle class American," who wrote a book "because I needed a hobby that would occupy my time in a productive fashion" (7).

Even arguments that spring from such modest intentions seek an audience, the bigger and more sympathetic the better. The success of a blog or a web page is usually calculated by the number of hits it attracts or the number of forwards it garners. Thus, as each of us competes for attention—from the basement blogger to the well-financed media company—we enter a situation in which we are not required just to make sense (if we are even required to do that); we have to entertain.

Public problems, public arguments

It would be a mistake to bemoan attention-getting without also acknowledging its necessity. Few large problems can be solved without public support, and—obviously enough—the public cannot support what it does not know about. Yet making the public aware of a problem is no simple task. Libby Lester, for one, discusses the complex, even treacherous, course that environmental issues have taken in order to reach the public through the media.

She argues that some descriptions of that process may be too linear, such as Downs' five-stage issue-attention cycle. In his description, an environmental problem first exists unnoticed by the public, even though it may already be quite serious. Next, the problem gains notice perhaps because of events that draw media attention. Typically, the public responds with both alarm and euphoria (because of prospects for solving the problem). However, that initial optimism soon gives way to more sober assessments. People begin to consider the financial cost of remedies and the personal sacrifices involved. In turn, the public becomes discouraged and attention wanes. Finally, although the public retains an awareness that it did not have before the problem entered public view, the problem garners less and less attention (Lester 44).

That cycle has a familiar and credible ring to it. However, Lester points out that the media environment is more dynamic and multi-faceted than such a step-by-step description suggests. To attract the public's interest, an environmental problem has to compete with other newsworthy problems and events. And that is a difficult competition. Some problems work synergistically with other newsworthy items. Some do not. Some problems are championed by organizations that help to keep them in the public eye. Some are not.

All environmental problems must compete for the limited attention the public has to offer. There simply is not room in the news day or in a human mind for all of the things that might be worthy of time and interest. Moreover, even if a problem reaches the public's eyes and ears, it can be transformed in unexpected ways. Lester points out that in Australia, a surge of interest in climate change was accompanied, to the dismay of some, by a discussion of expanding nuclear energy (46–47).

Such is the daunting challenge that must be surmounted by anyone who wants to bring an issue to the attention of the public. It's no wonder that not all media utterances are characterized by even tones. When we are faced with the need to be heard in a cacophonous room, the human tendency is to shout. Consider the words of the environmental activist George Monbiot, who writes,

> Every battle we fight is a battle for the hearts and minds of other people. The only chance we have of reaching people who haven't yet heard what we've got to say is through the media…. [T]he war we're fighting is an information war, and we have to use all the weapons at our disposal. Whether we use the media or not, our opponents will. However just our cause and true our aims, they will use it to demonize and demolish us, unless we fight back. Exploit the media, or they will exploit you! (Quoted in Lester 37)

Of course, Monbiot invokes the persistent metaphor Argument Is War. Yet he casts the metaphor in a particular light. For him, the war footing justifies more than just a hostile attitude toward intellectual and political rivals. It also justifies a no-holds-barred way of seeking attention.

In other words, as I noted in Chapter One, the metaphor Argument Is War shapes public discussion in several ways. It both describes and encourages the antagonism we see in much public argumentation. It also guides those who want to attract attention—not just arguers who adopt a warlike posture in order to be heard but also media-purveyors who see contentious argumentation as a reliable technique for expanding audiences.

Robert Reich, former Secretary of Labor in the Clinton administration, tells the story of a television appearance in which he discussed economic policies with someone from the other end of the political spectrum. After the first segment, he felt gratified at the amount of agreement there had been between him and his Republican interlocutor. But in his earbud, he heard the program's director telling him to be angrier. He protested. He didn't want to be angry. "Why be angry?" he asked. The answer was a pithy distillation of the attention imperative:

> [B]ecause you have hundreds of people—thousands, millions of people—who are surfing through hundreds of television channels, and they will only stop when they see a gladiator contest, a kind of a blood-letting, a kind of a mud wrestling.

I am reminded of an old phrase: *I've got a great idea. Let's you and him fight.*

Amid all of this jostling and quarreling, many voices in the climate change debate betray an almost desperate need to attract attention. Just consider the titles of these skeptical books and articles: *The Greatest Hoax: How the Global Warming Conspiracy Threatens Your Future; Eco-Tyranny: How the Left's Green Agenda Will Dismantle America;* and *The Hockey Stick Illusion: Climategate and the Corruption of Science.*

There's something jarring about hair-on-fire titles for books that address what is, at root, a scientific dispute. Skeptical books, articles, and websites shriek for attention by focusing on scandal, error, and corruption. They frequently rely on ridicule—like these titles advertised on the Heartland Institute's website: *The Mad, Mad World of Climatism* and *Roosters of the Apocalypse: How the Junk Science of Global Warming Nearly Bankrupted the Western World.*

Such books are about more than just ideological disagreement. They engage in *recreational* hostility. They make a game of opposition and outrage. They make ridicule fun. They promise and deliver a discourse of incitement that attracts an audience already hostile to the consensus view. Then they work hard at increasing that hostility through a disdainful prose style.

Consensus-friendly books and blogs tend not to be similarly inflammatory. A typical title would be the National Research Council's *Climate Change: Evidence, Impacts, and Choices*. Yet many titles seek attention by emphasizing risk—some would say "using scare tactics." For example: *The Climate Casino: Risk, Uncertainty, and Economics for a Warming World; Storm Warnings: Climate Change and Extreme Weather*; and *Storms of My Grandchildren: The Truth about the Coming Climate Catastrophe and Our Last Chance to Save Humanity*.

Thus, rather than a steady stream of ridicule or scandal mongering, supporters of the consensus give us a heightened perception of danger. The home page of *ClimateCentral.com*, a website run by mainstream climate scientists and communicators, flashes headlines such as "Global Heat May Be Hiding in Oceans"; "2013 Poised for Record Lows to Outpace Highs" [which supports rather than contradicts consensus science]; and "Scientists Say Global Warming Hard to Reverse." Skeptics are well aware of this rhetorical predilection and label people in the consensus alarmists.

I have no doubt that the climate scientists and those who support them are committed to providing factual information about the science and economics of climate change. But it seems there is no escaping the attention imperative, not even for the most serious voices.

Recreational hostility

The climate change debate has not reinvented the media and its techniques. Rather it participates in a media environment that all too often treats serious issues as fodder for entertainment. Even that is not entirely new. Debate has traditionally been both an intellectual exercise and a spectacle. Ask any forensic society.

Yet the current practice of presenting all issues as polarized and antagonistic is especially alarming to many (as I discussed in Chapter One) and is both catalyzed and exacerbated by the splintering of media technology—the proliferation of cable television channels, the rise of the Internet, and the consequent stratification of audiences. All too often, the attention imperative has a deleterious effect on the way climate change arguments are made. Their rhetorical timbre discourages genuine exchanges of ideas—which, in turn, shapes their content. Let me offer a few examples.

Bill Nye, the Science Guy

The first thing we should note about Bill Nye is that he is not, strictly speaking, a scientist—nor does he claim to be. His website lists three honorary Ph.D.s, but doesn't mention his bachelor's degree in engineering from Cornell University. He began his career as a mechanical engineer at Boeing, where he developed parts for the 747 (Schwartz). Now he describes himself as an actor and director.

He is best known in the United States for a popular children's program called *Bill Nye the Science Guy* that ran in the 1990s. Indeed, speaking to young people remains his passion. He recently told *The New York Times*, "There's nothing I believe in more strongly than getting young people interested in science and engineering—for a better tomorrow, for all humankind. I'm not kidding" (Schwartz).

In many ways, Nye is not a likely candidate to become a major voice in the climate change debate. His credentials and experience are not closely related to climate science. He is CEO of the Planetary Society, an organization of space enthusiasts whose mission statement does mention climate change. Moreover, though he is charming, he does not possess notable gravitas. He sports a floppy bow tie and looks as if he might, at any moment, offer to show you a card trick.

Yet he has established himself in the U.S. as the go-to debater of so-called anti-science figures. In 2014, he participated in a well-publicized debate about evolution with creationist Ken Ham, held at Ham's (in)famous Creation Museum in Petersburg, Kentucky, where dinosaurs are shown living contemporaneously with human beings in the Garden of Eden. Nye has also participated in a number of televised debates with climate change skeptics such as career denier Marc Morano and Congresswoman Marsha Blackburn of Tennessee.

"*Why him?*" we might ask. We would not have to search long for a plausible answer. Although Nye lacks the scientific bona fides of many working climate scientists, he has two things they do not: celebrity and the ability to perform with equanimity and wit in televised squabbles. And squabbles they are.

The general content of these climate change debates is predictable. Climate skeptics raise the question of the Medieval Warming Period, dispute the temperature record, and say that there is no scientific consensus about climate change. Nye patiently (but not too patiently) says that the Medieval Warming Period was a local phenomenon that affected just Europe. He assures his opponents that the Earth is, in fact, warming. He explains that, indeed, scientists do broadly agree about climate change. He frequently admonishes his opponents that the only way to discuss climate change intelligently is to look *at the facts*. They respond with a deluge of "facts" that he head-shakingly rebuffs.

While the points and counterpoints may be unfamiliar to many viewers, Nye and his opponents rehearse well-worn disputes between skeptics and supporters of mainstream climate science. The tone of the debate circumscribes its content. But it is not just the content of the debate itself that matters, anyway: It is at least as much the spectacle of the debate itself and the attention the debaters are able to attract.

One way to bring the attention-getting aspect of these debates into relief is to view them in the light of practical intertextuality. Intertextuality is often approached as a theoretical matter; it helps us to see connections between texts that are often unknown to us and sometimes difficult to discover. Bakhtin, for example, points out that almost unknown to us, every utterance carries traces of other utterances in a Great Chain of Communication. With the advent of the hyperlink, intertextuality is both concrete and impossible to miss. If you do an Internet search for Bill Nye and climate change, you will be presented with a series of texts and videos that demand to be viewed each in the context of the other. In fact, numerous videos are placed side-by-side on Nye's own website.

Thus, a web surfer who views Nye's debate with Congresswoman Blackburn is likely to also see Nye's appearance on John Oliver's cable comedy program (*Meet, Last*). The tone of that show is raucous and irreverent. Before introducing Nye, Oliver delivers a caustic monologue about climate change deniers. At one point, he praises the practice of talking about climate change as a current rather than a future problem. We cannot be trusted with the future tense, he says, because when we've been told about catastrophic harm to future generations, we have collectively responded, "F—— 'em!" That sets the tone for Nye's appearance.

Nye's role is to act as a prop in Oliver's critique of "balanced" debates. Oliver's complaint is that climate change is not controversial among scientists, yet it remains so on television, where climate change debates are presented one-on-one. Nye has been recruited because he is so often one of the two debaters. Oliver points out that a recent study has shown that 97 percent of scientists accept the main findings of climate science (see Chapter Five). So he proposes to hold a properly balanced debate. He brings out a skeptic to debate with Nye. The skeptic is quickly joined by two other skeptics. Then, for proper balance, Nye is joined by 96 scientists. Hilarity ensues (*Last*).

In general, the tone of Nye's debates is not comedic. Nonetheless, they are entertaining disputation. The audience tunes in not to become better informed about the science of global warming but to witness Nye as he vanquishes a climate change skeptic (for skeptics, it's vice versa). Consider the way Nye's relatively polite debate with Congresswoman Blackburn on the widely respected news program *Meet the Press* is characterized on Internet postings of the video. A sampling: "Marsha Blackburn Clashes with Bill Nye about Climate Change Debate"; "Marsha Blackburn Slams Bill Nye over Climate Change"; "Bill Nye Schools Marsha Blackburn on Climate: Stop Denying and Start Leading"; "Bill Nye Scolds Marsha Blackburn GOP Congresswoman on Global Warming."

Nye's debate with Marc Morano was less polite. It was held on CNN's *Piers Morgan Tonight*, rather than on a comparatively soporific Sunday morning news show. The tit for tat was contentious. Nye asks Morano if he agrees that carbon emissions are rising. Morano responds, "Sure. Carbon dioxide's rising. What's your point?" Nye discusses extreme weather events. Morano compares Nye's scientific reasoning to "the daily horoscope." Pummeled by Morano's relentless interruptions and rapid-fire recitations of talking points, Nye finally says with some exasperation, "I appreciate your yelling. That's good" (*Piers*).

The "yelling" was no less frequent on Nye's appearance on CNN's *Crossfire*. Nye was pitted against Heritage Foundation economist Nick Loris, who resolutely disputes the major findings of climate science from predictions of rising temperatures to the benefits of reducing carbon emissions. Conservative host S.E. Cupp cites a study showing that cows would emit more greenhouse gases in a year than the hotly debated Keystone pipeline proposed for the upper Midwest of the U.S. She then asks Nye if we should all become vegetarians. And so it went.

A striking feature of these staged clashes is how they circumscribe the content of the discussion. Because they are designed to emphasize dispute, they avoid areas of possible agreement. Indeed, they select participants who, in fact, do not agree on anything.

Furthermore, they reinforce the attention-getting practices of each side of the debate. *Crossfire's* S.E. Cupp challenges Nye on the "scare tactics" used by scientists, as well as the White House, to frighten people into action. Nye responds that climate change is serious business—that a proliferation of tornadoes in Oklahoma and the prospect of crop failures ought to scare us. She decries the "bullying" that the scientific community directs at those who do not believe them, which is a cue for Nick Loris to ridicule the scientific community's intelligence and character.

For the targeted viewership, it is probably riveting television. But it is not the kind of debate that needs to be had about climate change. It's no wonder that Gavin Schmidt of the Goddard Institute refused to participate in a debate on Fox News's *Stossel*. Instead, he appeared in sequential interviews on same program— first scientist, then skeptic, then scientist. Asked by host John Stossel why he refused the debate format, Schmidt responded, "I'm not interested in doing this because it's good TV. I'm interested in doing this because what we have discovered as a scientific community needs to be talked about" ("Green Tyranny"). Of course, the YouTube post that I viewed was headlined with the attention getter: "Climate scientist Gavin Schmidt runs in fear from a debate."

Masters of ridicule: Anthony Watt and Marc Morano

As of this writing, if you google *Watt's Up With That?*, you will see a partial subtitle: "the world's most viewed site on. ..." The site itself supplies the rest: "global warming and climate change." On the home page, prominently displayed on the right-hand sidebar, you see traffic statistics: 194,579,710 views (circa late July 2014). Of course, there are views and there are views. Some of those views are mine, and I didn't always linger for very long. Blog views should be taken with a pinch of the same salt used for interpreting inflated magazine circulations. But, still, 194,579,710 is a lot of traffic.

Why should *Watt's Up With That?* begin by touting how much attention it is able to attract? Surely there are other things to tout? It might tell you instead that the site is the most credible, the most comprehensive, the most accessible, or the most enlightening. But Anthony Watt, the former television meteorologist who runs the site, leads with the number of views for a good reason—not just to brag about the site's success in a competition for eyeballs. The attention imperative is not just about being heard; it's about supplying social proof you are worthy of being heard. To be heard is *ipso facto* to be credible.

That is surely why three of the four promotional quotes featured on the home page emphasize the site's large audience. From fellow skeptic Jonathon Mosely: "one of the most influential resources on global warming." Two of the quotes are, perversely enough, from spokespeople for consensus science. From environmentalist Fred Pearce: "the world's most viewed climate website." And from climate scientist Michael Mann: "flashy (apparently widely distributed)." The quotes from Pearce and Mann are especially strong because they are what lawyers call admissions against interest. Even those who oppose everything *Watt's Up With That?* stands for must admit that it attracts a lot of attention.

The spotlight on its large readership goes hand in hand with the site's other bids for credibility. On Anthony Watt's bio page, he strikes a neutral pose. He says he favors green issues and practices. He has solar panels on his house. He drives an electric car. We should trust him, goes the argument, because he is not just unbiased; he is predisposed to take the other side. He claims a super-neutrality.

But the rhetorical tone of the site is anything but neutral. *Watt's Up With That?* consists of links to articles penned by Watt and other skeptics. The titles of the articles are all adamantly anti-consensus. Many are vitriolic and *ad hominem*: "These Are the Sort of People We Are Up Against"; "Quote of The Week—The 'Lie Big' Law (or Why Can't John Cook Tell the Truth?)"; "Climate Spin—More Than Just a Game, It's 'Wheel of Gore.'"

It is no subtle observation to say that *Watt's Up With That?* is filled with hostile argumentation. Yet unlike the debates that feature Bill Nye, it cannot be likened to a boxing match. In a boxing match, opponents are in the ring together. Watt shows you only the punch, not the counterpunch. That tells us something about the kind of attention the site wants to attract. Its high number of views would mean far less if the site generated casual interest or mere curiosity. The site aims to incite animosity toward absent argumentative opponents. The attention imperative demands not just large numbers but intensity of interest.

It may be helpful to consider that in light of rhetorical theories of audience. Audiences cannot help but adopt a responsive attitude. Thus, competent writers and speakers aim to shape that response. With respect to writing, Walter Ong calls that fictionalizing an audience—the process of both imagining a desired audience and asking that audience to imagine themselves in that desired way. *Watt's Up With That?* casts its readers in the role of an intensely interested climate change skeptic, perhaps even an angry one, and asks them to become even more skeptical and angrier. It is difficult to read *Watt's Up With That?* any other way. To approach the site as someone who accepts mainstream climate science is to cast oneself as an outsider—an unintended, undesired audience.

Of course, the audience for *Watt's Up With That?* is not entirely fictionalized. As Andrea Lunsford and Lisa Ede explain, calling out to audiences is both pull and push. They accept the notion of an "audience invoked," a version of Ong's fictionalized audience. They also point out that the goals and interests of the actual audience—the audience addressed—always figure in. Clearly, *Watt's Up With That?* addresses an audience of actual skeptics. But, real as they may be, the site asks them to respond in that role alone and to respond fervently. To borrow a phrase from the American novelist Willa Cather, it asks them to become more like themselves.

And readers oblige. Consider the responses to posted articles. On one of my visits, the first article linked is "Introducing the *WUWT* CO_2 Reference Page," which argues that carbon emissions are not linked to increased temperatures. It includes a number of graphs, one of which shows five years of flat surface temperatures correlated with five years of continuing carbon emissions. The point is, evidently, to make the dubious claim that carbon emissions do not cause warming.

Readers of *Watt's Up With That?* are not just convinced by that claim; they are energized by it. Some responses are caustically ironic, such as this one: "It appears that the biggest contributors to global warming are NASA [National Aeronautic and Space Administration] and NOAA [National Oceanic and Atmospheric Administration]." Some argue in favor of emitting carbon, such as these: "Man is simply facilitating getting the CO_2 back into the atmosphere, whence it came," and "The more I learn about Climate Change, the more I realize that increased warmth and CO_2 concentration are a net benefit to the planet." Some are accusatory, such as this one: "The relationship between atmospheric CO_2 and the magnitude of USHCN [United States Historical Climatology Network] data tampering shows a 1:1 correlation."

In short, *Watt's Up With That?* attracts an in-kind response that is resolute and disdainful of mainstream climate science. We cannot assume, of course, that all of the thousands of viewers that the site attracts are as intensely supportive as those who post comments. However, unlike reader responses to controversial newspaper articles, where acrimonious debates between left and right thrive, *Watt's Up With That?* inspires readers not just to agree with each other but also to one-up each other in their ridicule of the absent opponent. In hopes of seeing what the site's dissenters have to say, I read through 433 reader responses for three articles posted on *Watt's Up With That?* (Watts "Global Temperature Update"; Watts "Get a Vasectomy"; "Just the Facts"). There were, in fact, some internecine skirmishes, some of them extended. But there were no dissenters. Everyone made it clear that they oppose what *Watt's Up With That?* readers call "warmists," "warmunists," and "climate scientologists."

Watt's Up With That? works hard to keep its audience's attention by adding articles daily, even hourly. For all of that effort, I should note, it makes for extraordinarily sluggish reading (for me). Many articles are filled with scientific jargon. Even that, however, works in favor of the attention imperative because it permits the audience to regard itself as scientifically literate and chiefly interested in "just the facts"—justified in the attention they give to the site.

Such a disinterested pose may not be as easy to maintain for readers of *Climate Depot*, the website published by Marc Morano, the indefatigable skeptic who debated Bill Nye on CNN, and a one-time aide to Senator James Inhofe. Morano's site is financed, in part, by such donors as Exxon/Mobil and the ultra-conservative Richard Mellon Scaife Foundation. Its home page is filled with headlines that make the site's political leaning unmistakable, blending accusations of environmentalists' ill will with evidence of their nefarious deeds. In August 2014, the featured headline is "U.S. Senate Report: Left-Wing 'Billionaire's Club Using Environmentalism to Control the U.S. Economy and Subvert Democracy.'" Below that are "A Dozen States File Suit against EPA [Environmental Protection Agency] Climate Rules"; "IMF [International Monetary Fund] Urges Higher Energy Taxes to Fight 'Climate Change'"; and numerous others with a similar political emphasis.

If *Climate Depot*'s political viewpoint is more transparent than that of *Watt's Up With That?*, its use of ridicule is much the same. Side by side with its political reports, it posts an article from right-wing *NewsBuster.com* that presents six scientific studies that sound, on their face, laughable:

1 Five Climate-Change Claims as Ridiculous as Sharknado[1]
2 No More Red Hair Because of Climate Change
3 "Some Experts" Claim 2008 Increase in UFO Sightings "Could Be Linked to Global Warming"
4 Senator Warns Winter Sports, Stadiums Threatened by Climate Change
5 Global Warming Will Make Earth Spin Faster
6 Italy's Pasta in Danger

Readers of *NewsBuster.com* (linked on *Watt's Up With That?*) greeted this story with gleeful ridicule. The item about a possible disappearance of red hair (because red hair may be an adaptation to cool cloudy weather) drew some banter about race—for example: "Omg [Oh my god] so the fight against Global Warming is really all about white people trying to keep the planet from going brown! It is racist to support Global Warming hysteria!" Another reader ridiculed the notion that global warming has wide-ranging effects: "Global warming makes milk go bad.... makes adults stupider.... makes scientist not able to tell the truth.... makes boats go faster.... makes the summer longer.... makes politicians more honest.... makes Lego more popular...."

Such ridicule can only thrive among like-minded people. The larger that group, the better. The more joy one takes in ridiculing a shared opponent, the better. In sum, the more attention and the more passionate the quality of that attention, the better.

The attention imperative in a flat world

Thomas Friedman is fond of telling us that the Internet has flattened the world, allowing obscure individuals and groups to be, in some instances, evenly matched with large corporations and governments. He makes a good point. But it depends. Individuals and small, poorly financed groups have a difficult time attracting enough attention to shape the debate. But they do participate.

A good example is the website *Catastrophe Map*. The publisher of the site and blog—and, like Anthony Watt, author of most of its content—is pleased to have a small but interested audience, which numbers in the hundreds not in the hundreds of thousands. He harbors no illusions that climate change or other environmental catastrophes can be avoided. He sees the corporate interests as too powerful and the general population's attention to environmental issues as too slight.

So *Catastrophe Map* leavens its commentary with layers of ironic humor and sardonic disparagement of anti-environmentalists. Its biography of Marc Morano reads, in part:

> As executive director of *ClimateDepot.com*, Marc Morano gets paid $150,000 a year to pretend that global warming is a scientific fraud. The people behind *ClimateDepot* are the Committee for a Constructive Tomorrow, who in turn get their money from ExxonMobil, Chevron and similar petrochemical types.
>
> Marc has no scientific or even journalistic training, but he does have a history with key deniers, the most prominent of whom is Senator "The Hoax" Jimmy Inhofe of Oklahoma. Morano also performs repeatable acts of public oral tribute for Heartland Institute, the folks who sponsored a Chicago billboard comparing climate change scientists to Unibomber Ted Kaczynski.
>
> Marc joined the world of right wing delusion working as Rush Limbaugh's producer. It was there he learned how to make stuff up.
>
> Our favorite quote:
>
> "Coal is the moral choice, particularly for the developing world...."

Such prose may, at first, seem to be a mirror image of *Watt's Up With That?* or *Climate Depot*. But *Catastrophe Map* has more in mind than that. It presents not just ridicule of climate deniers and other anti-environmentalists and more than just reports on fear-inducing environmental calamities. It also provides an instructive parody of the attention-getting techniques that characterize the climate change debate. Its ridicule is exaggerated and self-aware. Its alarmism (though earnest at root) points an amused finger at alarmism.

Consider the titles of its article headlines: "Keep Drillin' Boys! Atmospheric Carbon Levels Reach 400 PPM as Global Hydrocarbon PLUNDER-AMA Gathers Momentum" and "Given a Paradise, We Create a Barren, Degraded Hell Hole on Earth." Consider its major headings: "Toxic Apacalypse" and "Postcards from a Pissed-Off Planet." Consider the name of its companion blog: "Let the End Times Roll."

Note

1 *Sharknado* is a tongue-in-cheek movie thriller in which a massive shark-infested tornado destroys Los Angeles.

Works cited

Bakhtin, M. M. "The Problem of Speech Genres." Speech Genres and Other Late Essays. Trans. Vern W. McGee. Austin: U of Texas Press, 1986. 60–102. Print.
Catastrophe Map. n. pag., n.d. Web. 20 Aug. 2014.
Climatedepot.com. n. pag. Web. 2 July 2014.
Ede, Lisa and Andrea Lunsford. "Audience Addressed/Audience Invoked: The Role of Audience in Composition Theory and Pedagogy." *College Composition and Communication* 35.2 (1984): 155–71. Print.
"Green Tyranny." *Stossel.* Fox. 28 Mar. 2013. n. pag. Television. Transcript.
"Just the Facts: Introducing the WUWT CO_2 Reference Page." Watt's Up With That? Web. 11 Aug. 2014.
Lanham, Richard A. *The Economics of Attention: Style and Substance in the Age of Information.* Chicago: U of Chicago, 2006. Print.
Last Week Tonight. HBO. 11 May 2014. hbo.com. Web. 2 July 2014.
Lester, Libby. *Media and Environment: Conflict, Politics and the News.* Cambridge: Polity, 2010.
Meet the Press. NBC. 16 Feb. 2014. n. pag. Transcript. Web. 2 July 2014.
Noonan, Joseph Patrick. *Global Warming: Why You Should Be Afraid.* iUniverse, 2012. Nook file.
Piers Morgan Tonight. CNN. 4 Dec. 2012. n. pag. Transcript. Transcripts.cnn.com. Web. 2 July 2014.
Ong, Walter S.J. "The Writer's Audience Is Always a Fiction." *PMLA* 90.1 (1975): 9–21. Print.
Reich, Robert. "The Politics and Economics of Inequality." *Apenideas.org.* 30 June 2014: n. pag. Transcript. Web. 5 Aug. 2014.
Schwartz, John. "Firebrand for Science, and Big Man on Campus." *New York Times.* 18 June 2013: D1. Print.
Toulmin, Stephen. *The Uses of Argument.* Cambridge: UP, 1958. Print.
Watt's Up With That? Web. 11 Aug. 2014.
Watt, Anthony. "'Get a vasectomy to save the planet' guy calls for a Hurricane to hit the Caribbean." Watt's Up With That? Web. 11 Aug. 2014.
——. "Global Temperature Update – Still no global warming for 17 years 10 months." Watt's Up With That? Web. 11 Aug. 2014.

9   Chasing ice, chasing eyes

As much as some of us may wish it weren't, climate change's argumentative situation is—metaphorically speaking—war. In war, some weapons are more effective than others. So, I pose these questions: What single argumentative weapon packs the most force? What is its nuclear bomb?

In my estimation, the answer is the visual—the graph, the illustration, and most of all, the photograph. The hockey stick graph published by the IPCC crystallizes the rise in the Earth's average temperature in a way no set of figures ever could. *Time*'s 2006 photo of a polar bear stranded on a small patch of ice stirs our emotions in a way that no verbal or quantitative account of arctic melting could ever hope to ("Be worried"). Perversely glorious images of melting glaciers are so convincing to so many that the reality of climate change is, on that basis alone, beyond question.

However, it is not just the emotional or persuasive force of visuals that makes me want to call them the debate's most potent weapon—therefore, the one that deserves to be treated with the most caution. Climate change visuals are especially fraught because they are infused with all of the things that make the argumentative situation exceedingly difficult.

So far, I have discussed these difficulties one at a time. But we should not think of them as separate problems or as a causal sequence in which one problem leads to another. All of the problems are mutually exacerbating. For example, it would be harmful all by itself for people to find published facts untrustworthy. It is even more harmful, though, when people's doubts about facts are colored by motivated reasoning and confirmation bias. Each makes the other problem worse.

So it is with all of the problems I've raised: an uncertain stance toward science and its methods; a declining trust in facts; motivated reasoning and confirmation bias; values that unconsciously shape our reasoning and sort us into opposing camps; and an imperative to seek attention in public discussion. Separately, these things might be manageable. Together, they form a toxic argumentative stew.

Visuals in the climate change debate have embedded in them all of the problems I have already mentioned. They also have a particularly long reach and persuasive impact. In my opinion, they are the most important "weapon" in the climate change debate.

Chasing ice

In this chapter, I want to concentrate on a particularly elaborate yet representative example of the visual rhetoric employed by those who favor the consensus view, the 2012 film *Chasing Ice*. The film shows photographer James Balog as he produces time-lapse images of melting glaciers in Iceland, Greenland, Alaska, and Montana. It is a documentary of documentation. But it is more than that. The photographic evidence of glacial melting is disturbing, convincing, and extraordinarily beautiful. Reviewers came away from the film both wonderstruck and afraid.

Here is a sampling of reviewers' quotes posted on *RottenTomatoes.com*:

> Still an eco-sceptic? Clap your eyes on this lot. Awe-inspiring, terrifying, transcendently beautiful, and absolutely weighted with significance for the future of the planet. Trevor Johnston

> *Chasing Ice* is a grand adventure, a visual amazement and a powerful warning. Colin Covert

> The rapid disappearance of ice mountains, filmed over a period of years, is compressed through time-lapse technology into minutes and seconds. The speeded-up effect is harrowing and also, disturbingly, eerily beautiful. Peter Rainer

> On one hand, it's humbling to watch as a glacier the size of five football fields slumps into the ocean like a defeated whale, while on the other it's eye-opening to think about how cataclysmic the effects could be in years to come. Steve Carty

> It's like watching our world disappear. Philip French

I usually read the phrase "critics rave" with a suspicious eye. But when it comes to *Chasing Ice*, they really do.

But what kind of argumentative gesture are they raving about? At its core, *Chasing Ice* is about facts. Its aim is not to further an argument but to end a debate by presenting indisputable evidence that glaciers in Iceland, Greenland, Alaska, and Montana are melting at an unprecedented rate. Balog demonstrates this melting by compiling four years of time-lapse photography. Those compilations are shown near the end of the film. They are its climax and its point. If seeing is believing, Balog gives us no choice but to believe.

Of course, that evidence only takes up a minute or so. If the evidence alone were so powerful, it would be sufficient to post it online and allow the evidence to speak for itself. But *Chasing Ice* provides an elaborate framing of that evidence. It is not enough for us to recognize facts and revise our opinions accordingly. The film demands that we view the facts in a certain way. To paraphrase W.J.T. Mitchell, the pictures want something more from us.

If we take the film's initial one minute and twenty-seven seconds as our guide, it wants us to be afraid. The fearful tone is established immediately. The opening credits run only three or four seconds and are shown over a soundscape of thunder, a distant siren, and ominous music. We cannot ignore the aural and verbal contexts of images, especially the way they either reinforce or recast images' meanings. (For a discussion of the relationship between words and images, see Schriver.)

Immediately following the credits, we see a house ripped from its foundation and swept helplessly along by rushing floodwaters. It looks oddly small beneath an escarpment four times its height. Next, we are shown a graphic that depicts wildfires all across Texas followed by footage of raging flames. Then, it's a storm-chaser video of the tail of a large tornado and a sky filled with swirling debris. A moment later, it's Hurricane Irene's rushing waters and destroyed trees and property. Then, cracked earth caused by a drought in Nepal. Then, wildfires in Russia. Then, cars swept along by still more surging floodwaters. These are alarming images—*prima facie*. We don't really need the terror-inducing musical soundtrack for us to reach that conclusion.

But when we view them within the context of the film's narrative, raw fear is not quite the point. *Chasing Ice* is similar to other consensus-friendly visual rhetoric, which pursues a nuanced strategy of appealing to fear. The stranded polar bear on the cover of *Time* invites us to identify with the bear's predicament. The shrinking patch of ice stands for melting glaciers. And melting glaciers are a proxy for the collapse of the world. One response to these incitements might be panicked action. But people in the consensus are after something else—not just fear of a physical threat but fear of a mind-set that multiplies that threat.

Chasing Ice's opening images are intercut with narratives from news anchors and with hot debates between the skeptics and the proponents of climate science. The news anchors tell us that these extreme weather events are extraordinarily dangerous and expensive. We learn that rebuilding from Hurricane Irene is likely to cost seven billion dollars, that 2011 will be the most expensive year yet for weather-related damage, that Russian fires are a "horror," that the Nepal drought is of historic proportions, and that hurricane Irene's flooding is like nothing that's been seen before. To make the connection to climate change explicit, a talking head intones that 15 of the previous 20 years were the warmest on record. That's all quite disturbing.

But even the connection between global warming and extreme weather is not the thing we need to fear the most. Even as we witness what seems to be indisputable photographic evidence that global warming is already wreaking havoc, we encounter astonishing denials from skeptics and exasperation from supporters of the consensus view. Fox News commentator Sean Hannity says that no matter what the event—heat, cold, snow—"there's nothing that doesn't prove it's global warming." Actor Ed Begley Jr. shouts at Fox News personality Stuart Varney to stop denying the evidence for global warming. Glenn Beck pronounces that the only consensus is that there is no consensus. Comedian Lewis Black holds his head in his hands in frustration at such statements. And John Coleman, founder of the Weather Channel and confirmed skeptic, assures us that the ice caps are not going to melt and the seas are not going to rise. He promises that "twenty years from today I'll be the one that's laughing."

So the narrative is set. We need to fear climate change. But we already knew that. Science had already shown it beyond a reasonable doubt. The more immediate threat is obdurate denial. Enter James Balog.

We first glimpse him on a chilly shore in Iceland. There are no storms or floods or fires in sight. All is serene. He's dressed in winter clothes and laden with photographic equipment, SLR in hand. He and his assistant are discussing how he will capture the ice formations on film (or in pixels). Balog has very bad knees, and his assistant is concerned that he might slip and injure himself on one of the rocks scattered in the burbling water where he wants to stand. Balog insists that he must get these pictures. So he sends his assistant back to the car for rope. When he shoots his frames, the rope is looped around his waist as a safety measure. He's also removed his shoes because, as he explains, he knows he will get wet. Best to stand barefoot in icy water to take the photos.

The photos are stunning. We see them in a series of stills, punctuated with sounds of a snapping shutter. Who knew ice could be so magnificent? These photos want wonderment from us. And I can't imagine who would not grant it. But if the aim were just to capture aesthetically pleasing photos, the shoeless, cliff-hanging, death-defying Balog might just be a foolish risk taker. In *Chasing Ice*, he is a hero. He only faces danger for the good of others—for something larger than himself. His mission, we learn, is to document the disappearance of glaciers in the Arctic for the sake of all civilization.

Balog is well suited for the task. In interview snippets, he tells us that he was once a graduate student in geomorphology. But statistics and computer models were not "him." So he began photographing the natural world—specifically, the interaction between humans and nature. Of course, the environmental movement nearly always casts human influence on nature as destructive. His first major project was to photograph grisly scenes of hunting. We are shown his photos of bloody carcasses piled high—including those of baby seals. They repulse, and they are meant to repulse. Thus Balog is not a hero to all. He is a hero for his group—people whose chief moral foundation, above all others, is to prevent harm from coming to living things.

In that pursuit, Balog is like the archetypal hero Odysseus, both courageous and clever. The repulsiveness of the bloodied carcasses taught him that he needed photos of another kind, photos that attract. He has learned that he must heed the attention imperative. So when he turned to photographing endangered species, he presented them in a more "seductive fashion," to "engage people, pull them in." We are shown his extraordinarily beautiful photos of a lion, a leopard, a polar bear, a panda—lit like fashion models. We are shown exotic trees shot against gauzy white backdrops. Expert commentators—themselves shot in flattering soft light—testify to the power of Balog's work. Dr. Sylvia Earle, a *National Geographic* explorer, tells us that his photographs have the ability "to change the world."

Balog's photos either benefit or suffer from the tensions discussed so eloquently by Susan Sontag. On the one hand, Balog set out to record the world as it is. In his documentation of animal carcasses, he provided evidence of what he saw as misdeeds against animals—horrors. Without his photos, we might not believe it was ever so. As Sontag puts it, "Something we hear about, but doubt, seems proven when we're shown a photograph of it" (5). But, of course, a photograph is never just a record of reality; it is always an exercise of power over its subject. Sontag points out that "even when photographers are most concerned with mirroring reality, they are haunted by tacit imperatives of taste and conscience" (6). That is why, she suggests, photographers in America's Great Depression took dozens of shots of sharecroppers until they achieved a depiction that "supported their own notions of poverty, light, dignity, texture, exploitation, and geometry" (6). Surely, Balog considered such things in photographing animals that had been killed.

But the camera does not treat all subjects equally. Some photographers, Sontag says, have followed Walt Whitman's view of beauty, a democratic view of beauty that sees everyone and every moment as worthwhile. However, a more commonly held view is that a beautiful photo is a photo of something beautiful. Balog seems to have adopted that view. He began to stage beauty for the sake of his photographs. With ingenious manipulations of lighting and backdrops, he created images of animals that can rightly be called "ecoporn" (see Welling).

What Balog's photos want from us, then, is complicated. When he shows us melting glaciers, he wants our aesthetic awe, but only in order to activate our Care/Harm moral foundation regarding the climate. He wants our rapt amazement but he also wants our fear. And as the opening of the film shows us, the fear of climate change, by itself, is not sufficient. We must also be afraid of climate skeptics' stubborn ignorance.

That's why his extraordinarily beautiful images of ice formations and his time-lapse photos of glacial melting occupy so small a proportion of the film. These images are clearly the film's high points—its main attraction. Some would call them transcendent because, even as we see the ice disappearing, the images seem to demand of us something spiritual. Skeptics would probably see this treatment of images as a form of worship—evidence that there is, indeed, an environmentalist religion.

Yet the images are not, themselves, the story of the film. The story is about the process that attends factuality. Most of the film bears witness to Balog's meticulous, tedious, and authentically audacious effort to provide us with irrefutable evidence of Arctic melting. His still photos provide the proof. But the film provides proof that the images of melting ice are, indeed, proof (compare J. Doyle).

The unfortunate fact is this: Even images of melting glaciers do not have uncomplicated probative value. Skeptics have pounced on Al Gore's dubious use of glacier images in the film version of *An Inconvenient Truth*. They were, it turns out, computer simulations first used in the climate-change thriller *The Day*

After Tomorrow (Champion). And that has lent credence to allegations of photo trickery of all kinds.

To see photography as direct evidence of anything may be naïve. Yet even the most sophisticated visual rhetoricians have had to acknowledge that photography invites uncomplicated expectations. Susan Sontag makes that point powerfully by pointing to a moment in history when photographs were absent from public discourse:

> One would like to imagine that the American public would not have been so unanimous in its acquiescence to the Korean War if it had been confronted with photographic evidence of the devastation of Korea, an ecocide and genocide even more thorough than those inflicted on Vietnam a decade later. (18)

Sontag adds that such photographs were absent because a dominating ideology prevented them from being present—and that even when photographs of Vietnam's atrocities were seen, they were only powerful because they were viewed through an intellectual lens that permitted the American public to understand them as atrocities, rather than as justified acts of war.

In a similar if less visceral vein, Roland Barthes refers to the "myth of photographic 'naturalness.'" He acknowledges both the strength and complexity of our ordinary expectations of photographs:

> The type of consciousness that the photograph involves is indeed truly unprecedented, since it establishes not a consciousness of the *being-there* of the thing (which any copy could provoke) but an awareness of its *having-been-there*. What we have is a new space-time category: spatial immediacy and temporal anteriority, the photograph being an illogical conjunction between the *here-now* and the *there-then*. It is thus at the level of the denoted message ... that the real *unreality* of the photograph can be fully understood. ... For in every photograph there is the always stupefying evidence of *this is how it was*, giving us, by a precious miracle, a reality from which we are sheltered. (44)

What strikes me most about both Barthes's and Sontag's observations is not that photographs are more complicated than everyday notions would suggest (that's true of everything). Indeed, since the time in which they wrote, digital technology has made most of us understand, as a practical matter, that photographic evidence is almost never a straightforward thing. Rather, what strikes me is that the credulous view of photography that they take pains to debunk still survives. Without a naïve expectation, accusations of photographic trickery make no sense.

It may be that the confidence we place in visuals, especially photographs, makes us all the more disappointed when our confidence is betrayed. That is historically so, at least. A 1998 *Atlantic Monthly* article titled "Photography in the Age of Falsification" provides a shocking—shocking!—chronicle of faked nature photography. One shocker is about a photo of polar bear reclining on its belly as it gazes at an iceberg. The "shot" was used in a photography company's advertisement, and it ran in *National Geographic*. The problem is, the bear turned out to be a resident of an Ohio zoo. To make matters worse, it was even faked wrong. The setting was in the Antarctic, where there are no polar bears. Photoshop was the culprit here. Yet we can't blame digital technology for everything. Did you know that, in the 1950s, Disney faked the iconic mass suicide of lemmings—literally chasing them off a ledge with a bulldozer? (Brower)

Indeed, concerns about photo fakery are far from new. Arthur Conan Doyle's 1912 novel, *The Lost World*, hinges on a dispute about a scientific expedition's photographs of modern-day dinosaurs. One character muses, "Was it possible that in this age of ingenious manipulation photographs could be accepted as evidence?" In the novel, the answer turns out to be no. Today, the answer is much the same—for photos and for all kinds of visual displays, including drawings, charts, and graphs. Visuals are often the most compelling ways to make a point. But they are also a great temptation for chicanery (Allen, Bryan, Yoos).

Chasing Ice's remedy is to show the photographic process in meticulous detail. We see Balog in his studio discussing the challenge of creating time-lapse technology. Surprisingly—to Balog, not just his audience—the equipment had to be created especially for his project. After all, Balog's cameras have to function in extremely inhospitable conditions in the northernmost reaches of the planet. In the course of things, he and his team deal with the failure of timers, equipment damage perpetrated by birds and foxes, cameras getting buried under 20 feet of snow, and frigid batteries exploding inside of cameras.

At one point, Balog is reduced to tears over these mechanical setbacks. All of his work, he says, is worth nothing without the photos. But that is only a moment of despair. He is persistent. Obsessed. In a narrative that covers several years, we see him and his assistants installing cameras—drilling into rock to secure camera braces and guy wires, scaling snowy slopes to check to see if the cameras have been shooting, and celebrating when they work. The cameras ultimately collect more than 100,000 frames.

So when we see those frames (in quick time-lapse succession toward the end of the film), they want quite a lot from us. Not just for us to accept them as evidence of melting. Not just our aesthetic wonderment. But our appreciation for the lengths to which scientific heroes had to go in order to gather them.

Balog and his team—but especially Balog—go through quite a lot. Over a soundtrack of cold wind and pulsating music, we see the team pushing their car out of a snowy stream; we see the team traveling by dog sled—soon capsized; we see them navigating snowy nights with head lamps; we see them traveling in a helicopter whose engine fails—the dominant image not of the pilots calling for help but of Balog's stoic reaction; we see the team trudging through snow blown horizontally; and we see their orange tent unmoored and blown like a beach ball across the snow. In perhaps the most dramatic sequence of the film, we see Balog and a team member repelling into a seemingly bottomless crevasse in the ice, secured only by ropes and spiky shoes, so that Balog can shoot a still of his unapologetically terrified assistant—to establish scale.

Indeed, the visual and verbal story of the film is only in small part about the images that Balog captures and very much about images of Balog capturing them. By the time we see a montage of his spectacular photos, we cannot separate their otherworldly beauty from the sacrifices Balog undertook to get them. In interview snippets, his wife and daughter testify to his persistence and passion. We see him suffer excruciating pain in his failing knees, see him wheeled into an operating room, and finally see him traverse the snow and ice on crutches.

But if the film focuses on the sacrifices that made Balog's images possible, it is only to show that Balog and his team are focused on the scientific facts. Key images of glacial melting are shown to us in two main ways. First, we see them as they are gathered. That is, we don't see the images unfiltered; we see the photographer seeing them. When we are at last shown the time-lapse sequences of extraordinary glacial melting—the film's *pièce de résistance*—we see them in the context of Balog's slide presentations in front of an audience. We see the photographer seeing others see his images. The witnessing is never separated from the witnessed.

Second, we are not left to interpret the images for ourselves. Often, their significance is demonstrated for us using graphic overlays. The glaciers photographed by Balog are melting very quickly. In just six months, the Solheim Glacier in Iceland melts so dramatically that it reveals a mountain ridge that had been entirely hidden. To make that point clear, a superimposed orange line traces the shape of the mountain on the image of the glacier before it melts: what was is seen in comparison to what will be. The visual process is the inverse of what Edward Tufte advocates, giving two-dimensional data displays a third dimension (*Envisioning*). Here, three-dimensional photographs are turned into two-dimensional charts and graphs.

Similar graphical overlays are used frequently in the film—such as hash marks to show that an ice peninsula is the length of five football fields. The scale is difficult to perceive without familiar markers such as people or buildings or trees. So when we are shown ice breaking off the tip of a melting glacier—the largest "calving" event ever captured on film—we are not left to guess how large that event was. We are provided with an overlay of the tip of Manhattan, which is—almost incomprehensibly—similar in area to the ice chunk that breaks away and goes out to sea. More striking yet, the ice is nearly three times the height of New York's skyline.

All of this bolsters the credibility of Balog's photographic documentation. Graphic overlays are part of the visual language of science. They work hand-in-glove with testimonials from authorities who vouch for the reality of anthropogenic climate change—scientists, an insurance executive, a *National Geographic* editor, and the former head of the CIA, James Woolsey. And James Balog himself.

In the end, it might well be said that Balog's still images themselves make no argument at all. In fact, I would not dispute what David Fleming argues so elegantly—that pictures simply cannot articulate the basic elements of an argument: a well-defined claim attached to evidence. But the images in *Chasing Ice* are not just visual evidence appended to verbal arguments. They are, as Roland

Barthes might argue, saturated with the connotations of the time and place in which they are viewed.

We cannot view Balog's images outside of the context of climate change's argumentative situation or outside of environmentalist discourse. When we witness Balog's photographic witness of breathtaking ice formations, we are reminded of the Earth's purity, of its sanctity, and of the duty we owe it. Even the images of the Earth succumbing to our carbon dioxide desecration remind us of the transcendence of nature. Yet it is also scientific proof.

At last, as the film closes, we see the time-lapse montages of glaciers disappearing before our eyes. By then, the montages are not just evidence that global warming is upon us. They are evidence that the skeptics are wrong. They are evidence that our own doubts are unfounded.

Balog says in the film that he once had doubts about global warming. He thought it was unlikely that humans were capable of altering the physics and chemistry of the entire planet, that climatologists' computer models might well be unreliable, and that their results were probably filtered through the hyperbole of activism. He was what I would call a fair-minded skeptic. But now—with his own eyes and through his own camera lens—he has seen the evidence. And we have seen him see it.

The melting of the glaciers is awe-inspiring not just because of the speed and scale of the destruction. And not just because of the photographic beauty. The melting is awe-inspiring because to witness the melting is to understand death—to experience the uncomfortable relationship between being and nothingness that once fascinated Jean-Paul Sartre. Balog is, perhaps, no Sartre, but he sums up that relationship well as he stands in the snow, holding in his fingertips the memory card of one of his time-lapse cameras: "The memory of the camera is the memory of the landscape. That landscape is gone. It may never be seen again in the history civilization, and it's stored right here." He can feel that "time is clicking" and knows "we need to get these cameras out here."

And yet

Chasing Ice is far from the only demonstration that climate change is real. And Balog is far from the only hero in the argumentative situation. In *An Inconvenient Truth*, Al Gore casts his old Harvard professor, the climate scientist Roger Revelle, as a hero. Al Gore himself has been cast as a hero. He was given the Nobel Peace Prize for drawing attention to climate change. But one faction's hero is another faction's villain. It seems no amount of heroism and no amount of visual evidence can settle the dispute over climate change.

That is the great irony of *Chasing Ice*. Even though it claims to have, once and for all, delivered definitive proof, Balog muses early in the film about the futility of scientific argument. We are still arguing about "a minor thing called evolution," he observes. The lesson he draws is not that the climate change dispute can or will be settled. It's that, unlike other scientific disputes, this dispute cannot wait for further argument: "We don't have time."

Even so, no weapon in this argumentative war has been powerful enough to secure a certain victory for the consensus view. Not even Balog's nuclear bomb.

Works cited

Allen, Nancy. "Ethics and Visual Rhetorics: Seeing's Not Believing Anymore." *Technical Communication Quarterly* 5.1 (1996): 87–105. Print.

Barthes, Roland. "The Rhetoric of the Image." *Image, Music, Text.* New York: Hill and Wang, 1977. Print.

"Be Worried. Be Very Worried." *Time.* 3 Apr. 2006. Cover.

Brower, Kenneth. "Photography in the Age of Falsification." *The Atlantic* May 1998: 92–111. Print.

Bryan, John. "Seven Types of Distortion: A Taxonomy of Manipulative Techniques Used in Charts and Graphs." *Journal of Technical Writing and Communication* 25.2 (1995): 127–79. Print.

Champion, Sam. "Realistic Good and Bad Science; Legitimate Science in TV and Film." *20/20.* ABC News. 18 Apr. 2008. Abcnews.com. Web.

Chasing Ice. Dir. Jeff Orlowski. 2012. DVD. Submarine Deluxe.

Doyle, Julie. "Seeing the Climate?: The Problematic Status of Visual Evidence in Climate Change Campaigning." *Ecosee: Image, Rhetoric, Nature.* Ed. Sidney I. Dobrin and Sean Morey. Albany: SUNY, 2009. 279–98. Print.

Fleming, David. "Can Pictures Be Arguments?" *Argumentation and Advocacy* 33.1 (1996): 11–22. Print.

Schriver, Karen A. "The Interplay of Words and Pictures." *Dynamics in Document Design.* New York: Wiley Computer, 1997. 361–441. Print.

Sontag, Susan. *On Photography.* New York: Farrar, Straus and Giroux, 1977. Print.

Tufte, Edward R. *Envisioning Information.* Cheshire, Conn.: Graphics Press, 1990. Print.

Welling, Bart H. "Ecoporn: On the Limits of Visualizing the Nonhuman." *Ecosee: Image, Rhetoric, Nature.* Ed. Sidney I. Dobrin and Sean Morey. Albany: SUNY, 2009. 53–77. Print.

Yoos, George. "How Pictures Lie." *Rhetoric Society Quarterly* 24.1–2 (1994): 107–119. Print.

10 How should we argue?

Robert Frost wasn't sure how the world would end—with fire or ice—but thought that either would suffice. It's hard to top Frost for wit and rhyme. But on this subject, I side with my fellow Illinoisan, Carl Sandburg, who wrote more optimistically: "A baby is God's opinion that the world should go on" (7).[1]

In that spirit, let me end on a hopeful note. It may seem that argumentation holds little promise when it comes to climate change. It is up against so much. In fact, some of the most important participants in the climate change debate place their hopes in non-argumentative solutions. Anthony Giddens, for example, thinks what will ultimately work best are "convergences"—policies not directed at slowing climate change, but which have the side effect of reducing carbon and methane emissions. Former EPA (Environmental Protection Agency) head Christine Todd Whitman, a Republican who is deeply concerned about anthropogenic climate change, says, "I'm starting to move away now even from talking to people about climate change as a major issue and, say, how about clean air. ... I don't want to argue with you about whether humans are the cause of it or not."

But for all of the things that work against reasonable deliberation about our warming planet, there is still no insurmountable reason to think that argumentation will ultimately fail. What I want to offer in this final chapter is not a remedy for all that is wrong with today's argumentative situation. Rather I want to suggest a way of thinking about how we should argue in light of all that currently plagues the climate change debate. Moreover, although climate change is, in my estimation, the most important issue of our time, it is not the only important issue and not the only debate that is subject to all of the troubles I have discussed. Thus, I hope that my observations may have some broad application.

Here are some of the questions I think we should ask about the argumentative situation surrounding climate change and, indeed, the argumentative situation all around us.

Is it ethical to change other people's minds?

As I mentioned at the start, many scholars of writing and argumentation have profound misgivings about the very idea of changing other people's minds. It seems to them coercive or at least manipulative. Gearhart, for one, has characterized all acts of persuasion as "violence." So critics of persuasion advise softer forms of arguing. Their proposals have important nuances of difference. But whether the proposal is called Irenic or Rogerian or cooperative—whether we are asked to play Peter Elbow's "believing game" ("The Believing Game"), to adopt Jim Corder's "emergence toward the other," or to engage in Sonja Foss and Cindy Griffin's "invitational rhetoric"—all of the proposals are rooted in the same impulse. They ask us to be open minded, to question our own certainty, to be guileless, to be patient.

We underestimate those things at our peril. Indeed, I have deep reservations about debate for the sake of debate, about exhorting young writers to "take a side," about posing as the only one who knows what is right. There can be something corrupting about taking a public stand. In *Influence: The Psychology of Persuasion*, Robert Cialdini explains how those who would shape our behavior extract public statements from us. They do that because they know something about how we typically operate: Once we say something where others can hear it, we are psychologically inclined to stand by what we've said. In fact, we are likely to harden in our beliefs once we put our public imprimatur on them. Psychologists sometimes call this "escalation of commitment."

In addition, from a strictly practical perspective, most questions require openness because the answers can't really be known, which is why rhetoricians, starting with Aristotle, have identified deliberative rhetoric as one of the subject's major divisions. We engage in public deliberation when answers to our questions are not clear and, perhaps, can never be clear. It's more productive in those cases for us to reason together. None of us is smarter than all of us.

But then we come to climate change. Except in the sense of truly *radical* doubt, we do not have good reasons to question what climate scientists are telling us. Partly, that's because they have already reasoned together on our behalf. Partly, it is because they are only telling us what is likely to be correct—what is probable enough to justify action. All of their conclusions are accompanied by an escape clause. When the data changes, their predictions will be revised accordingly. Partly, it is because scientists only express certainty about particular kinds of questions. Much remains to be debated in the deliberative fashion, such as how to manage the social disruption that will follow on the heels of large climate disruptions.

Yet the part climate scientists are certain about is quite compelling. Consider some of the warnings included in a recent report published by leading climatologist James Hansen and his colleagues. Regarding sea level:

[T]he uncertainty is not about whether continued rapid CO_2 emissions would cause large sea level rise, submerging global coastlines—it is about how soon the large changes would begin. ... The carbon from fossil fuel burning will remain in and affect the climate system for many millennia, ensuring that over time sea level rise of many meters will occur—tens of meters if most of the fossil fuels are burned. That order of sea level rise would result in the loss of hundreds of historical coastal cities worldwide with incalculable economic consequences, create hundreds of millions of global warming refugees from highly-populated low-lying areas, and thus likely cause major international conflicts.

Regarding the extinction of species:

> [The IPCC] estimate[s] that if global warming exceeds 1.6°C above preindustrial, 9–31 percent of species will be committed to extinction. With global warming of 2.9°C, an estimated 21–52 percent of species will be committed to extinction. … If we drive many species to extinction we will leave a more desolate, monotonous planet for our children, grandchildren, and more generations than we can imagine. We will also undermine ecosystem functions (e.g., pollination which is critical for food production) and ecosystem resilience (when losing keystone species in food chains), as well as reduce functional diversity (critical for the ability of ecosystems to respond to shocks and stress) and genetic diversity that plays an important role for development of new medicines, materials, and sources of energy.

Regarding climate extremes:

> Heat waves lasting for weeks have a devastating impact on human health: the European heat wave of summer 2003 caused over 70,000 excess deaths. This heat record for Europe was surpassed already in 2010. The number of extreme heat waves has increased several-fold due to global warming—and will increase further if temperatures continue to rise.

Regarding human health:

> The IPCC projects the following trends if global warming continues to increase, where only trends assigned very high confidence or high confidence are included: (i) increased malnutrition and consequent disorders, including those related to child growth and development, (ii) increased death, disease and injuries from heat waves, floods, storms, fires and droughts, (iii) increased cardio-respiratory morbidity and mortality associated with ground-level ozone. While IPCC also projects fewer deaths from cold, this positive effect is far outweighed by the negative ones.

Given such dire predictions, I think we are faced with an argumentative imperative: When it comes to the climate change's main point of disagreement, it is more ethically fraught to argue in an uncertain way than to use all of our powers of persuasion. In fact, I think we can go a step further. We are well justified in imputing moral shame to those who doggedly take the other side (a category that does *not* include fair-minded skeptics). It has been done before. The world is better off because people argued against slavery, against Jim Crow, against apartheid, against genocide.

To recognize an argumentative imperative is not to set aside what has been conventionally recognized as ethical argumentation: honest claims, genuine evidence, sound reasoning, and plain talk. But is that kind of ethical argumentation enough?

What do we expect from audiences?

We would gain a lot of ground if we could truly count on what is conventionally expected from audiences. That is, it would help if audiences measured factual arguments by factual yardsticks alone. As I have said in this book, however, that is not how people usually operate, not even fair-minded skeptics. People tend to believe that they are objective finders of fact. But they are not.

Writing scholars and rhetoricians have shown us that writing and talking of all kinds—not just arguments—can only be produced and received competently by audiences who share values and practices with others in their professional communities or social groups. Enculturation into a group is what allows us to construe what is credible and what is worthy of attention. Stephen Toulmin recognized that when he explained that claims are supported by (often tacit) warrants—the underlying assumptions of a group. Similarly, a long list of genre researchers have demonstrated the power of coming to know what the discourse community knows (for example, Berkenkotter and Huckin; Devitt; Swales).

However, the climate change debate points to something more than that. The climate change debate reveals fissures between groups that are deep, resilient, and only partly conscious. What this calls for, I think, is a different set of expectations of audiences and, along with that, a different kind of audience analysis. To put it another way, we need to think searchingly about when and why people change their minds. After all, people *do* change their minds. Don't they?

James Balog, for example, says in *Chasing Ice* that he began as a climate change skeptic. He once thought—just as many skeptics continue to think—that humans' impact on the planet is too small to affect the overall physics and chemistry of the planet. He suspected—as many skeptics still do—that computer models were not a reliable enough tool to predict the climate's future. And he suspected—just as many skeptics maintain today—that the discourse surrounding climate change was "some kind hyperbole that was turning this into some kind of activist cause."

Of course, it bolsters Balog's credibility to say that he was not always a climate change believer—that he became convinced by evidence, not by inclination. Yet if anyone were ever poised for a change of mind, Balog would be a likely candidate. He was a nature photographer whose life's work was already closely aligned with environmentalism. His guiding metaphors and moral foundations made him receptive to the arguments of climate scientists, a fact that is demonstrated amply by the fervor with which he took up the cause of preventing global warming.

More surprising are conversions against expectations. Consider theoretical physicist, and one-time recipient of Koch brothers funding, Richard Muller. He wrote in a 2012 *New York Times* op-ed:

> Call me a converted skeptic. … Last year, following an intensive research effort involving a dozen scientists, I concluded that global warming was real and that the prior estimates of the rate of warming were correct. I'm now going a step further: Humans are almost entirely the cause. ("Conversion")

He went on to describe his Berkeley Earth Surface Temperature Project, which answered to his satisfaction the most compelling skeptical arguments. It relied on actual temperatures and CO_2 records, not on computer models; it ruled out the effect of urban heat centers by replicating results with rural data only; it used statistical correlations to rule out possible causes of heating, such as solar variability and world population growth; it used data from all weather stations, not a select 20 percent; and it eliminated the possibility of human bias by automating its processes. After all of that, Muller concluded that the only possible explanation for global warming is human activity that puts too much CO_2 into the atmosphere.

His conversion was greeted with much celebration. Bill Clinton called Muller his "new climate change hero" (van Diggelen). But it's not clear how dramatic the conversion actually was. In the very same op-ed in which he announced his change of mind, Muller listed a striking number of things about which he had not changed his mind in the least:

> I've analyzed some of the most alarmist claims, and my skepticism about them hasn't changed. Hurricane Katrina cannot be attributed to global warming. The number of hurricanes hitting the United States has been going down, not up; likewise for intense tornadoes. Polar bears aren't dying from receding ice, and the Himalayan glaciers aren't going to melt by 2035. And it's possible that we are currently no warmer than we were a thousand years ago, during the "Medieval Warm Period" or "Medieval Optimum," an interval of warm conditions known from historical records and indirect evidence like tree rings. And the recent warm spell in the United States happens to be more than offset by cooling elsewhere in the world, so its link to "global" warming is weaker than tenuous. ("Conversion")

That hardly represents a new alignment with climate scientists' general view.

To muddy the waters even further, it's not even clear that his claim to have previously been a skeptic holds much water. Judith Curry, the mainstream climate scientist who has worked the hardest to keep one foot in the skeptical camp, discusses Muller at length on her blog. She quotes him as saying that he was never a denier, not even a skeptic, more of an "agnostic."

Taking my cue from one of the reader-responders on Curry's blog, I read the climate change section of Muller's *Physics for Future Presidents*, published in 2008, four years before his "conversion." Muller didn't sound like much of a skeptic in those pages. He did take issue with what he calls political exaggerations about climate change. He was critical of Michael Mann's hockey stick graph. But, by and large, he argued the consensus case for climate change, indeed fully endorsing the IPCC's conclusions and their manner of expressing them. He wrote the following:

> Here is a little game I've played that illustrates how political exaggerations misrepresent what the IPCC says. I tell a colleague I think there's a 10% chance that none of the global warming is caused by humans. Then I ask, "Based on that, do you consider me to be a skeptic on global warming?" The answer always comes back yes. But by that criterion, the entire IPCC is a global-warming skeptic. (*Physics* ch. 5)

Muller seems only to be concerned about careless statements, not about climatologists' consensus. If he had been doubtful about human-caused climate change (that is, more doubtful than the IPCC), he would probably not have written at length about how to solve global warming, as he did in this book, and his main recommendation would not have been to curb Chinese emissions of CO_2.

Yet I am not debunking Muller's claim to have changed his mind. Indeed, I am more than willing to give him what I earlier called a truth discount. For all his protestations about speaking cautiously, Muller often writes for the general public in a provocative manner. His book titles include *Physics for Future Presidents*, *Energy for Future Presidents*, *The Instant Physicist*, and *The Sins of Jesus* (which is a novel that re-imagines Jesus in what I gather is an unconventional way). I take his conversion story to be of a piece with other benign bullshit that we encounter every day.

So I don't doubt that Muller *did* change his mind about climate change. I believe that his study did convince him more fully of things he once doubted, at least to some degree. That seems to be how changes of mind work. They are not usually dramatic one-eighties; they are revisions of thought that take place within the narrow parameters of existing belief.

So it is with James Lovelock, the author of *The Revenge of Gaia*, which I discussed earlier. In 2012, about the same time that Richard Muller became a celebrated convert to the consensus view, Lovelock was being congratulated by skeptics for admitting that he was wrong about climate change all along. This much is true: Lovelock did repudiate his most alarming language about an impending climate disaster. But his heart remained in roughly the same place it had always been. He said in an MSNBC interview, "We will have global warming, but it's been deferred a bit." He also said that humanity should still do its "best to cut back on fossil fuel burning" (Johnston).

What we can expect from audiences is something less than the Enlightenment ideal. Still, it is not too much to hope that some people will change their minds, especially when those changes occur within individuals' and groups' established boundaries. That means that the audiences most convinced by an argument are, if not the already persuaded, the already persuadable. Fortunately, that may be good enough if people who hold the consensus view find a way to appeal to a broad set of values.

Is there a fair way to frame an argument?

In the climate change debate, it seems that no accusation goes unmade or unanswered and that neither of the entrenched sides has any hope of convincing the other. However, it would not be accurate to say that the sides are—to use an over-used phrase—"talking past each other." Rather, they are talking *about* each other for the sake of an audience of third parties.

In many cases, that third-party audience is the proverbial choir. That choir is already predisposed to accept the general thrust of the argument. But that doesn't render the argument useless. Preachers sermonize to the choir in order to strengthen their belief, as well as to supply them with the fine grain of the argument. That is certainly so when environmentalists publish arguments about the urgency of climate change for an audience of people who already accept the idea that humanity is generally harmful to the Earth. It's equally true when skeptics speak to those who see the Earth primarily as an economic resource.

But argumentation should also do more than further enlighten the already enlightened. If its aim is not radical conversion, then it should at least aim for mind changing among as broad an array of people as possible. That is where framing seems particularly important.

George Lakoff has a rooting interest in the Democratic Party, and he has a festering disappointment in his party's inability to frame arguments convincingly. His notion is that most arguments are won or lost before the particulars are laid out because key concepts are often "framed" in ways that evoke powerful, usually unconscious, metaphors. For example, it is not just Republican orthodoxy that all taxes are "burdens"; it is a metaphor shared, in varying degrees, by people across the political spectrum. It tells us that paying for government weighs us down (*Don't Think*). That frame was extended quite effectively in Ronald Reagan's phrase "getting the government off of our backs"—which evoked the image of the government physically oppressing us. Once such metaphoric frames take hold, it is difficult to counter them. The frame creates a sort of attentional blindness and thus hides opposing views.

Lakoff is right to admire Republicans' framing skills. But liberals have succeeded in framing issues also. Martin Luther King made it possible for Americans to think differently about race by framing skin color as separate from the essential person: "the content of our character, not the color of our skin." More recently, attitudes toward gay marriage in the United States have changed so spectacularly that many states have made it legal, which seemed impossibly far off only a few years ago. That change was accompanied by a phrase that framed gay marriage in a new way: marriage equality. No value runs deeper in American culture than equality.

I don't mean to suggest that small changes in frames do all of the work of persuasion. We can't forget about the civil rights marches and demonstrations of the fifties and sixties or decades of work done by the gay rights movement to bring gays and lesbians out into the open. Surely, many Americans were poised for a change of mind when they came to see that gays and lesbians were not threatening strangers but their friends, neighbors, and family members.

Yet framing is far from insignificant. In 2011, a Rutgers-Eagleton poll found that 52 percent of New Jersey respondents favored gay marriage. But asked whether they favored marriage equality, the percentage rose to 61 percent. When it comes to political decisions, 52 percent is a squeaker, but 61 percent is a landslide.

Climate change has also been strategically framed. The phrase *climate change* was crafted by master framer Frank Luntz, a Republican consultant who is responsible for phrases such as *death tax* (instead of inheritance tax), *oil exploration* in Anwar (rather than drilling), and the language used in Newt Gingrich's contract with America. In 2002, Luntz wrote a memo to the White House explaining that the Republicans were losing the public relations battle over global warming and argued that the phrase *global warming* was part of the problem (Ball). It sounded too scary. *Climate change* sounded more natural and gradual. (He also argued that the Republicans' best defense against a growing consensus about global warming was to claim that scientists were not, in fact, in agreement.)

Climate change has now become the standard term for rising global temperatures. Although its interpretation has surely evolved since Luntz first recommended it, the term can still sound less frightening than global warming. It is sometimes used with an adjective: *dangerous climate change*. David Orr, the Sierra Club, and others prefer *climate disruption*. It occurs to me that global warming sounds fairly benign compared to, say, *global heating*. Nonetheless, neither *global warming* nor *climate change* evokes a fundamental value. The difference between the terms is only in how they calibrate the urgency of the danger. That's not irrelevant. Yet, as we've seen, it's not what really divides people about—well, let's call it *planetary broiling* for variety.

Climate change has also been framed in other ways. In fact, what may seem to be specific policy arguments about climate change function also as frames. When skeptics say that proposals such as a cap and trade scheme or a carbon tax will create an unfair economic burden on working people, they are not just making a claim that can be supported or refuted with evidence, but they are also setting the parameters for what matters in the debate (Nisbet). It casts climate change as a financial problem rather than an existential threat, and what ought to be over-riding long-term necessities are subordinated to short-term cost-benefit analyses. Those who oppose action on climate change see the problem of climate change (if they accept that problem at all) as less important than preventing an unduly slowing economic growth or imposing a tax burden.

On the other side of the debate, those who accept climate change frame the discussion as a matter of extreme danger. Trailers for Al Gore's film *An Inconvenient Truth* promised to be "the scariest movie you will ever see." *Time's* image of a stranded polar bear was headlined "Be Worried. Be very worried." This frame highlights genuine dangers. Because of the panicked tone in which it is expressed, the frame also provides an opening for the accusation of alarmism (Nisbet).

Additionally, the terms *skeptic* and *denier* frame the debate so that it emphasizes a dispute about the role and credibility of science. As we've seen, people who accept the scientific consensus often call their opposition flat-earthers. In some cases, the term may be well deserved. But it also frames the argument in a way that focuses on scientific certainty. Skeptics and deniers have made effective use of the counter-frame of *uncertainty* (Nisbet).

The climate change consensus is also associated with the environmentalist frame of natural purity, which tells us that almost all human interference with nature is harmful and that whatever emanates from nature is sanctified. This purity/sanctity frame sometimes reveals itself in talk of CO_2 as a *pollutant*. Indeed, it revealed itself especially vividly in President Obama's 2008 victory speech, "We will be able to look back and tell our children that … this was the moment when the rise of the oceans began to slow *and our planet began to heal*."

I would suggest that nearly all of the ways climate change is framed—by skeptics and by those who accept the scientific consensus—tend to perpetuate the current impasse because the frames cater strongly to the values of those who reside at one end or the other of the ideological spectrum. Consensus arguments, in particular, are not framed in a way that is likely to appeal to a broad audience. Indeed, spokespeople for the consensus tend to ignore the importance of framing altogether. They tend to make the Enlightenment-inspired error of believing that if you present credible facts in a logical way, audiences can be counted on to draw the right conclusions.

But making specific suggestions about fair and effective framing is a tricky business. The truth is, I can't make suggestions with confidence. When Frank Luntz makes his recommendations, he bases them on extensive interviews, focus groups, surveys, and high-tech measures of people's attitudes toward particular phrases and ideas. Recently, even Luntz has become discouraged. He finds the nation so divided that he feels he has reached the limits of his powers to make a difference (Ball). If he is not equal to the task of uniting people, perhaps I am not either.

Nonetheless, it's worth considering that there may be other ways to frame the problem of global warming and climate change. One way to do that is to consider the larger question of how we frame the environment. George Lakoff has argued that the environmental frame tends to configure the environment as something we live within—something separate from us. But we are not separate from the environment; we are inextricably a part of it. Likewise, environmental harm and economic harm are typically understood as separate spheres. But, as Lakoff points out, they are rooted in the same cause: greed. The result of unregulated greed, he writes, is "toxic assets and a toxic atmosphere" ("Why It Matters" 77). Lakoff's proposed frames may seem familiar. Like other environmentalists, he emphasizes connection and systematicity. Yet his suggestions have an important difference: they do not impel us to figure humanity as inherently harmful to the Earth.

If Lakoff's proposal to reframe the environment and its relation to ourselves turns out to be too heavy a lift, it might at least be useful for those in the mainstream to talk less of humanity as a disease or as agents of harm and to talk more about the human capacity to solve problems. Indeed, the climate scientist Mike Hulme points out that the ability for humans to affect the climate for the better has historically been viewed positively.

Rather than talk about *healing* our planet, which casts it as weakened—infected with the disease of humanity—perhaps those who hold the consensus view should talk about *repairing* our planet or *managing* our climate, which casts the climate as something for which we have responsibility and, importantly, our effect on it as potentially positive. That framing is not far different from what E.O. Wilson has proposed in *The Creation*, in which he urges religious believers and non-believers to come together around the idea of stewardship of the Earth.

Another way of looking at framing is to think about problem-setting. In a now classic essay, Donald Schön argues that the metaphors we use to describe problems act as problem-setting frames. Thus, they often prescribe (and proscribe) the solutions we are likely to consider. He observes, for example, that if we describe slums as a *blight* or a *disease*, the solutions we are most likely to consider are surgical. Similarly, in relation to environmental problems, Brendan Larson discusses the way some problem-setting frames can be harmful, such as the frame *invasive species*. That frame encourages a fearful and often militaristic attitude toward nature. Because invasive species are usually those introduced by people, it also encourages a view of nature that excludes human beings. In turn, it affects the way research funding is allocated and how the environment is managed.

I have some reservations about the way the problem of climate change has been framed, beginning with the broad phenomenon itself. As I said above, climate change was introduced as a euphemism for global warming, and *climate change* is sometimes rhetorically intensified as *dangerous climate change* or *climate disruption*. However, in the climate change frame, humans are relegated to the background. To be concerned about the climate is mainly to be concerned about the earth or the planet. But in a nontrivial sense, the planet is not the problem.

As my science-minded friends sometimes point out to me, the Earth's climate has changed a great deal over its 4.5 billion year history. The Earth itself is resilient. It has been very cold and very hot, very dry and very wet. It has, as Elizabeth Kolbert reports, seen mass extinctions. Nevertheless, the planet survives. The problem for most of us—the reason climate change keeps us awake at night—is that human beings are far more vulnerable than the planet.

Climate is important to us mainly because we—us personally, our children, our grandchildren—require a climate that will allow us to live comfortably or live at all. Although I do not make light of environmentalists' desire to heal the planet or dispute an ecosystematic conceptualization of the planet, I do suspect that when it comes to focusing people's attention on rising temperatures, the key point is not that the planet will suffer, not that many species are likely to go extinct, but that *our* species will find it increasingly difficult to live on Earth. One problem leads to another. When the climate is disrupted, the consequence is the destruction of the places we live and grow our food. As the late comedian George Carlin once joked (except that he wasn't quite joking), *the Earth is not going anywhere. We are.*

How can we phrase climate change in a way that brings humans into the frame pithily and memorably? I don't have that answer. But it does seem to me *that threat to human habitation* is more to the point than *threat to the planet*. It seems to me that wanting *to heal the planet* is not as pertinent to most of us as needing *to save our home*. Likewise, it may be more to the point for us to speak not about *preserving the environment*, which calls to mind the wilderness (which is indeed important), but rather to emphasize *protecting our cities and towns and farmland*.

Similarly, I have reservations about the terms *skeptic* and *denier*. They seem to point only indirectly to the problem of maintaining a suitable climate for human beings. When people are overly skeptical of scientific findings, the consequence may not just be inaction but even acceleration of the activities that are causing global temperature changes. Skepticism and denial are not the problem per se; they are the cause of the problem.

So I wonder if the word *skeptic* lets the opposition off too easily. Skepticism, after all, is generally regarded as useful. Rightfully so. No class of people is more skeptical than scientists. Furthermore, *denial* is cast as a mere escalation of skepticism. But it isn't really the same at all. Denial is not the vigorous examination of evidence but instead a refusal to believe what is patently so. Furthermore, both terms frame the debate in terms of acceptance of facts—as a question of certainty or uncertainty. That is precisely the debate that climate change skeptics and deniers prefer to have.

The so-called climate change skeptics and deniers (who are not the same as fair-minded skeptics) are really supporters of carbon pollution. At this juncture, to perpetuate the argument about climate change is to actively support excessive burning of carbon, the negligent release of carbon through deforestation, the negligent release of methane through accidental or collateral leaks, and the willful ignoring of natural feedbacks that release carbon into the atmosphere as the Earth warms.

Should skeptics and deniers be called carbon addicts or some such disparaging term? Perhaps so. But whatever the precise phrase, it would be more direct and it would define the problem more accurately if they were challenged not about their attitudes toward science but instead about their attitude toward *climate negligence*.

In addition, it seems problematic to cede the framing of the climate problem by (over)using an economic frame. It is true, of course, that climate change already costs us a lot of money and will cost us more in the future. It is probably also true that green technologies can generate a lot of wealth. However, to make economics the chief frame for viewing climate change seems rhetorically risky to me. The problem is not how much climate change will cost us or how much money we can make in addressing the issue. The problem is that we cannot afford continuing climate change at any price.

Whether or not these or some other frames might ultimately be effective, I cannot say. But I am sure of two things: Paying attention to how framing excludes and attracts is essential to better argumentation. Paying attention to framing is essential to our becoming aware of the values that we genuinely hold.

To be as clear as possible, I am not advocating manipulation. Some think, for example, wordsmiths like Frank Luntz take the science of linguistic influence too far. That is, I would point out, also one of the main criticisms of rhetoric as an art. In *On Rhetoric*, Aristotle said that people have ideas that rhetors should heed. He said, for example, that people believe slaves only tell the truth under torture. Appealing to hideous beliefs is not what sound arguers do—that is the work of demagogues. But there is such a thing as framing with a genuine heart. And there is such a thing as being more aware than we usually are of how we are framing our arguments.

What is the role of sounding the alarm?

In *The Sixth Extinction*, Elizabeth Kolbert tells us that a mere hundred million years from now, our greatest accomplishments will be reduced to a residue about the thickness of a cigarette paper—our sculptures and libraries and monuments (and, I would add, our theme parks and Walmarts and strip malls) (105). So when we think about climate change, maybe we should just shrug and say, "What's the fuss?" But I think most of us want to strive for survival—not just for our own personal survival but also for the survival of human civilization. For us, climate scientists and activists have described a future that we could not possibly want for our children and grandchildren. Our best minds have raised an alarm. And it has been oddly ineffective.

I have spent many pages trying to explain why we are so divided on the question of climate change, which is a way of explaining why so many of us are unalarmed. Still, there are some helpful ways of thinking about the role of alarm itself.

In the spring of 2013, several reports on American attitudes toward climate change were published by the Yale Project on Climate Change Communication and the George Mason University Center for Climate Change Communication. If the aim is to construct a solid public consensus about climate change, the news from their surveys is not good. Only 49 percent of Americans attribute global warming to human causes. Given that low percentage, it follows that only 51 percent of Americans are either somewhat or very worried about climate change (37 percent and 14 percent, respectively) (*Climate Change in the American Mind* 3).

Some of the Yale/George Mason findings help to explain the public's surprising lack of alarm. To begin with, in keeping with the arguments I've made in this book, perceptions of the risk of climate change track very closely with people's ideologies. Beyond that, there is something unalarming about the timing of the risks associated with climate change. People tend to see the risk of climate change, even if it is real, as distant in space and time. Only 40 percent of Americans believe that they themselves will be harmed by climate change; 68 percent believe that future generations will be harmed (*Climate Change in the American Mind* 9).

The immediacy of the threat is very important in shaping public attitudes. The Yale/George Mason surveys show that Americans' acceptance of climate change waxes and wanes in keeping with press coverage and extreme weather events. Acceptance peaked in 2007 and then dropped precipitously by 2010. During that time, news coverage of climate change declined dramatically (by as much as two-thirds), largely because economic news filled the pages and airwaves. Acceptance of climate change began to rise again in 2012, a year in which there were many extreme weather events that could be connected to climate change, including Hurricane Sandy. In the fall of 2012, a robust 67 percent of Americans accepted that climate change was happening (regardless of its cause). By the spring of 2013, though, with fewer extreme weather events in the news, that number had dropped to 63 percent (Leiserowitz).

Clearly, the more immediate the risk and the more publicity the risk receives, the more public opinion turns in favor of mainstream climate science. That, I believe, should give us some optimism about the effectiveness of argumentation. Given the tilt in opinion in the aftermath of extreme weather events, it may be premature to dismiss the effectiveness of mainstream scientists' and their supporters' efforts. Because of digital technology, arguments are archived and interlinked and accessible—awaiting the moment when they will become useful. They are also filtered so that those who are unlikely to master—or even hear of—the intricacies of such things as IPCC assessment reports are familiar enough with key points that they can make good judgments when events prod them.

On that point, the Yale/George Mason surveys provide a ray of hope. In the spring of 2013, 29 percent of Americans believed they could easily change their mind about climate change. The people most certain of their beliefs were those who accept the reality of climate change, not those who doubt it. Among those who accept climate change, 60 percent were sure of their conclusions. Among doubters, the number was less than half, only 46 percent (*Climate Change in the American Mind* 5).

A hopeful metaphor for argumentation

This book has been largely concerned with public opinion, but it's also important to think about argumentation in smaller contexts, such as among friends and family. As Anthony Leiserowitz of the Yale Project on Climate Change points out, the most public voices are not always the most influential. When people are asked who would be most likely to convince them to take action about climate change, the top answers do not include the President or renowned activists or climate scientists. They are inclined to listen to voices much nearer to home—close friends and family members. It should be encouraging to know that the fate of the planet doesn't rest only with the public voices so much at odds with each other. Even less amplified voices, such as yours and mine, can matter a great deal.

It might be worthwhile, then, to think about what metaphor might express a hopeful view of argumentation. Certainly, the old standby, Argument Is War, will not do. It places far too much emphasis on the head-butting that takes place between contending, immovable sides. At the same time—at least to my ear— some of the alternative frames do not call to mind genuine, urgent argumentation. Argument as Invitation. Argument as Collaboration. Argument as Art. Argument as Prayer.

Instead, I think about something Pete Seeger once said. Asked if his songs really make a difference, he said they surely do, although he couldn't prove it. Imagine a seesaw weighted down at one end with a basket of rocks. On the other end, up in the air, is a basket partly filled with sand. Each song adds another spoonful of sand to that basket. People may look at it and say, *What a waste of time! The sand leaks out as fast as you put it in!* But, said Seeger, if you have enough people with spoons, someday that seesaw will tilt the other way.

So it is with the arguments we make.

Perhaps our capacity to argue is God's way of saying that the world should continue.

Note

1 Strictly speaking, these words are spoken by a character in the novel *Remembrance Rock*, not by Sandburg himself.

Works cited

Aristotle. *On Rhetoric: A Theory of Civil Discourse*. Trans. George A. Kennedy. New York: Oxford UP, 1991.

Ball, Molly. "The Agony of Frank Luntz." *The Atlantic Monthly*. 6 January 2014. Theatlantic.com. Web. 6 Jan. 2014.

Berkenkotter, Carol, and Thomas N. Huckin. *Genre Knowledge in Disciplinary Communication: Cognition, Culture, Power*. Hillsdale, NJ: L. Erlbaum Associates, 1995. Print.

Chasing Ice. Dir. Jeff Orlowski. 2012. DVD. Submarine Deluxe.

Cialdini, Robert B. *Influence: Science and Practice*. Boston, MA: Allyn and Bacon, 2001. Print.

Climate Change in the American Mind Americans' Global Warming Beliefs and Attitudes in April 2013. Yale Project on Climate Change Communication, George Mason University Center for Climate Change Communication. Web. 11 Aug. 2014.

Corder, Jim W. "Argument as Emergence, Rhetoric as Love." *Rhetoric Review* 4.1 (1985): 16–32. Print.

Curry, Judith. "The 'Irresistable' Story of Richard Muller." *Juditycurry.com*. 4 Aug. 2012. Web. 6 Jan. 2014.

Devitt, Amy J. "Generalizing about Genre: New Conceptions of an Old Concept." *College Composition and Communication* 44.4 (1993): 573–86. Print.

Elbow, Peter. "The Believing Game—Methodological Believing." Paper presented at the Conference on College Composition and Communication, New Orleans, Louisiana, Apr. 2008. Web. 11 Aug. 2014.

Foss, Sonja K., and Cindy L. Griffin. "Beyond Persuasion: A Proposal for an Invitational Rhetoric." *Communication Monographs* 62.1 (1995): 2–18. Print.

Gearhart, Sally Miller. "The Womanization of Rhetoric." *Women's Studies International Quarterly* 2.2 (1979): 195–201. Print.

Hansen, James *et al. Assessing 'Dangerous Climate Change': Required Reduction of Carbon Emissions to Protect Young People, Future Generations and Nature.* 3 Dec. 2013. Web. 11 Aug. 2014.

Johnston, Ian. "'Gaia' Scientist James Lovelock: I Was 'Alarmist' About Climate Change." NBCNews.com. 23 Apr. 2012: n. pag. Web. 1 Apr. 2014.

Kolbert, Elizabeth. *The Sixth Extinction: An Unnatural History*. New York: Henry Holt, 2014. Print.

Lakoff, George. "Why It Matters How We Frame the Environment." Environmental Communication: A Journal of Nature and Culture 4.1 (2010): 70–81. Web. 2 July 2014.

Larson, Brendan. *Metaphors for Environmental Sustainability*. New Haven: Yale UP, 2011. Print.

Leiserowitz, Anthony. "Climate Change in the American Mind: Anthony Leiserowitz." Video. Vimeo.com. 11 June 2013. Web. 4 July 2014.

Muller, Richard. "Global Warming." *Physics for Future Presidents: The Science behind the Headlines*. New York: W.W. Norton, 2008. Chapter five. Kindle edition.

——. "The Conversion of a Climate-Change Skeptic." *New York Times*. 30 July 2012, A19. Print.

Nisbet, Matthew C. "Communicating Climate Change: Why Frames Matter for Public Engagement." *Environment: Science and Policy for Sustainable Development*. March–April 2009, n. pag. Web. 29 Jan. 2014.

"Rutgers-Eagleton Poll Finds New Jerseyans Still Favor Legalizing Gay Marriage." *Rutgers Today*. 28 October 2011: n. pag. Web. 1 June 2014.

Sandburg, Carl. *Remembrance Rock*. New York: Harcourt, Brace, 1948. Print.

Schön, Donald A. "Generative Metaphor: A Perspective on Problem-Setting in Social Policy." *Metaphor and Thought*. Ed. Andrew Ortony. 2nd ed. Cambridge: Cambridge University Press, 1993. 134–63.

Swales, John M. *Genre Analysis: English in Academic and Research Settings*. Cambridge: Cambridge UP, 1990. Print.

Toulmin, Stephen. *The Uses of Argument*. Cambridge: UP, 1958. Print.

van Diggelen, Alison. "Bill Clinton Praises His New Climate Change Hero." *Huffington Post*. 1 Dec. 2012. n. pag. Web. 6 Jan. 2014.

Whitman, Christine Todd. Interview by Chris Hayes. *All In*. MSNBC, 22 Apr. 2014.

Epilogue

Global climate change calls for a coordinated global response. Yet it seems to me that no genuine effort is likely to be made unless individuals come to terms with how a warming planet touches their own lives and how it relates to their own practical and ethical thinking. So, I want to share what I have personally come to think and feel about climate change.

At the start of this book, I referred to the nuclear threat that cast its shadow over my childhood in the 1960s. I said it was surprising to me that our atomic finale may well be preempted by a different kind of disaster—a cataclysm arising not from the malevolence of war but instead from humanity's technological progress. I am attached to the analogy between nuclear war and climate change, but not uncritically. I think it helps us to recognize the scale and urgency of climate change. Yet, as with all analogies, it only goes so far. The contrasts between the nuclear threat and the climate threat may tell us something as well.

One obvious difference lies in attitudes among the most powerful. Nuclear war was always something that nuclear powers urgently wanted to avoid. In the aftermath of Hiroshima and Nagasaki, all of those who had the capacity to wage nuclear war understood its horrors and wanted no part of them. After all, the point of superpowers' nuclear arsenals was largely to deter a nuclear attack. Other than providing an uneasy version of national security, nuclear war had no advantages.

Climate change is nearly the opposite. To use an atomic-age metaphor, the fallout from rising temperatures may end up displacing more people, spreading more disease, and destroying more cities and croplands than nuclear weapons ever will (not that the nuclear threat has disappeared entirely). Yet the nations that bear the chief responsibility for causing climate destruction are not, so far, urgently focused on deterrence. Surely that is because the process of causing climate change has so many advantages that can, in fact, seem indispensable.

The comparatively sluggish response to climate change probably arises from another difference: the way the destruction proceeds. A nuclear strike arrives with a blast like no other blast—horrifyingly destructive and horrifyingly visible. Its devastation then continues with the delayed effects of invisible, tasteless, and odorless nuclear radiation. Climate change is just the opposite. It has arrived stealthily. We can't see, smell, or taste additional carbon dioxide in the air. Only later on will its effects become shockingly apparent.

It's surely easier to focus our attention on an immediate explosion than it is to focus on a hidden time bomb, especially if we're not sure how big the ultimate explosion will be. A number of people have observed that because the brunt of climate change will be felt far in the future and because most of climate change's catastrophes will be concentrated on poorer populations, rich countries have difficulty taking it seriously (Jamieson, Hulme). I cannot dispute that point. Indeed, I take it to be true. But I think it's a mistake to settle on that as a full explanation of why the debate about climate change persists. The notion that distant threats must fail to spur us into action—or that immediate attractions always trump longer-term concerns—certainly runs counter to my own response.

I had a basic, layperson's understanding of climate change before I began reading in earnest for this book. I was concerned about global warming, but I also had questions that kept me from thinking in urgent terms. My thinking began to change when I learned more about the extreme damage that may well occur; when I better understood that there is a lag time between greenhouse gas emissions and their effects; when I learned more about the feedback mechanisms that multiply the effects of greenhouse gas emissions; and when I considered the centuries-long damage that greenhouse gas emissions will do. Awareness of these things—indeed, exposure to convincing arguments—has made me more concerned, not less, about the prospects for disaster.

My concern is not abstract, either. It is not a vague concern for unborn multitudes, but a visceral concern for my children and for the children they may have. The largest disruption from climate change may lie in the future, but not so far off that I cannot feel strongly about it. Some effects of climate change will not be seen until the twenty-second century. But that only heightens my sense of responsibility. It is one thing to cause damage that will soon pass, something much worse to cause permanent harm. (Jonathan Haidt would point out that the Care/Harm moral imperative dominates my thinking. When it comes to climate change, it does indeed move to the front of my mind.)

In short, climate change may be for the most part a future prospect, and future problems can usually wait for future solutions, but not in this instance. The threat of severe climate disruption is not that far off, and our duty to future generations in extreme circumstances is not easy for me to ignore. It is a part of my ethical framework, and I suspect—and hope—that better argumentation about climate change can bring our responsibilities into focus for many others, too.

My own feeling of responsibility is, in part, a consequence of the most dire predictions. Climate change skeptics often cite alarmism as a fatal flaw in the case for action. There is, indeed, such a thing as unfounded alarmism in human affairs. A well-respected geologist I happened to meet one summer assured me that human-caused climate change is quite real, yet she criticized scientists and activists who talk only about worst-case scenarios. Humans have a tendency, when faced with grim predictions, to say, "Let's all calm down. Things will turn out."

But that's not how the most worrisome predictions have affected me. In that respect, the analogy between climate disruption and nuclear holocaust is a very strong one. Nuclear war between superpowers may always have been, and I hope still is, unlikely. But the consequences of nuclear war would be so devastating that even a relatively small likelihood is unconscionable. That is also true for catastrophic climate change.

Some might caution me to remember that climate change will not *necessarily* wreak havoc equivalent to nuclear detonations. I accept that point. Scientists have described a range of possibilities for our climate future. Yet, for me, that's a double reason to favor strong, prudent action to curb greenhouse emissions. If the most likely effects of climate change are serious but not catastrophic, it still makes good sense to stave off as many serious consequences as possible. Failing to do that only makes the most severe consequences more likely. And the worst-case scenarios are likely enough to matter. How can we accept even a small chance of an enormous—and preventable—tragedy?

If I have come to feel a sense of urgency about climate change, it is not because the case for it is simple. True, the images of climate change that we know best are convincing partly because they simplify and thus clarify. When we are shown an image of a polar bear stranded on an ice floe, we may take that to be a full-enough explanation of what global warming can mean. When we are shown city-sized portions of glaciers dropping into the Arctic waters, the case for global warming seems plain enough. The poles melt, our shores flood. It's not hard to understand.

For me, though, those images are not as illuminating as events that are somewhat harder to capture in a single image. Climate change is characterized most of all by complexity, contingency, and uncertainty. So I think it is worth the effort to view climate change in light of its inherent complications.

A good example is occurring not so far from my home. In some parts of the northern U.S. and Canada, moose populations are declining rapidly. Scientists cannot say precisely why this is happening, but the likely explanations are rooted in a single cause—climate change. Overall, the United States is about two degrees Fahrenheit warmer than it was 40 years ago. In the northern U.S., recent decades have seen shorter winters and longer, hotter summers. Moose are particularly sensitive to temperature changes, so they act as the canary in the coal mine, so to speak.

Yet—though climate change may be a single root cause—the threat to moose populations manifests itself in different ways. In the White Mountain area of New Hampshire, the number of moose has dropped from 7,500 to 4,500 and many moose have become infested with deer ticks, which multiply in warmer weather. A single moose can have as many as 150,000 ticks, and some are so bothered by them that they rub themselves hairless. Tick-infested moose sometimes die from anemia as ticks feed off their blood, and at other times the moose die as a result of hypothermia because they lack the warming protection of their fur (Fears).

North of the U.S. border, in British Columbia, ticks have also been a problem. But an even larger problem seems to be an increase in pine bark beetles. These beetles kill off parts of the forest and leave moose vulnerable to predators such as wolves and people (Robbins). In Minnesota, one moose population has dropped from 8,000 to 3,000, another from 4,000 to just 100. The main culprits for those populations are liver flukes and brain worms that are carried by snails that thrive in warmer weather (Robbins).

In all of these areas, the rise in temperature itself can be a direct stressor for moose, who expend needed energy trying to stay cool and, in some cases, die from exhaustion. Still, in each region the onset of climate change has its own contours. To complicate matters further, the die-offs may not be a consequence of climate change alone. Scientists are considering a wide range of possibilities.

We really cannot think usefully about climate change without thinking through its complexities and even its paradoxes. Consider the moose and wolves of Isle Royale in Lake Superior, between Michigan and Ontario. They have been the subject of a scientific study that has now been running for more than 50 years. Because of Isle Royale's relative isolation—it can only be reached by air or boat—it has provided a particularly interesting example of how a large mammal and its chief predator achieve a balance without human interference (see Knott-Ahern *et al.*).

Moose first arrived on Isle Royale in the early twentieth century, and the population has climbed and plummeted several times for reasons unrelated to climate change. When the moose first arrived, they were unmolested by wolves, so they fed happily on balsam fir and grew in number—until they had depleted the fir they needed to sustain themselves. The moose population declined accordingly. Eventually, though, the fir rebounded and so did the moose. Then the same thing happened again. When wolves arrived from Canada in the 1940s, they kept the moose population at a sustainable size. A workable ecological balance was established.

Other things interfered, though—usually having to do with humans. There was a drop in the wolf population when people brought domesticated dogs onto the island and many wolves died from a dog-borne virus. Now, a more pervasive kind of human activity is affecting the island.

As the climate has warmed, the water temperature of Lake Superior has risen by about four degrees Fahrenheit. The ice bridges that once formed every year or two between the island and Ontario now form only once every 15 years. So the animals and plants on Isle Royale are left to survive changes in the climate on their own—with no new wolves or moose migrating in or out.

The result has not been good for wolves and is not likely, ultimately, to be good for moose. With no new wolves coming onto the island, the wolves have become inbred, most of them exhibiting a congenital spine deformity. As of 2014, the wolf population had dwindled to eight—down from about 40 at its peak. The consequence has been a spike in the number of moose, a near doubling in the last few years. Yet seemingly good news for moose will likely turn sour. Without a major predator to keep their numbers down, they will surely—as they have done before—overfeed on the balsam fir that covers the island. Moose populations will drop and so will populations of other animals that depend on the forest (Vucetich and Peterson). Climate change has cascading effects.

In 2013, scientists were debating the question of whether or not to introduce new wolves onto the island. In general, scientists do not want to interfere with the course of nature. The predominant ethical stance is to alter ecosystems only when humans have directly put it out of balance. But some—including the scientists who have dedicated their lives and careers to studying the ecology of Isle Royale—began to favor bringing in new wolves (Vucetich, Nelson, Peterson). In yet another twist in the story, however, 2014 brought a harsh, cold winter. Ice bridges formed. As of this writing, it's not clear whether that means new wolves will move onto the island or whether the remaining wolves on Isle Royale will move away.

I think Isle Royale helps us to make sense of the larger picture with respect to climate change in a number of ways. To begin with, the fluctuation of animal populations is not a new phenomenon. The effects of climate change are blended with natural cycles. In addition, the precise effects of climate change are not easy to predict. Scientists did not know in advance that the wolf population would drop so low. Finally, some of the short-term effects may seem, at least for some animals and plants, either beneficial or not harmful. Complexity, contingency, uncertainty.

Yet, in the end, climate change will not be good for Isle Royale. Without regular ice bridges, the moose and wolves are vulnerable to ever rising temperatures. It occurs to me that we are on an island of our own. Where is our ice bridge?

Works cited

Fears, Darryl. "With Warmer Winters, Ticks Devastating N.H. Moose Population." *Washington Post.* 9 Aug. 2013: n. pag. Washingtonpost.com. Web. 2 July 2014.

Haidt, Jonathan. *The Righteous Mind: Why Good People Are Divided by Politics and Religion.* New York: Pantheon, 2012. Kindle file.

Hulme, Mike. *Why We Disagree about Climate Change: Understanding Controversy, Inaction and Opportunity.* Cambridge, UK: Cambridge UP, 2009. Kindle file.

Jamieson, Dale. *Reason in a Dark Time: Why the Struggle against Climate Change Failed and What It Means for Our Future.* New York: Oxford UP, 2014. Kindle file.

Knott-Ahern, Louise, Rod Sanford, Dave Wasinger, Reid Williams. "Silence of the Wolves: A Lansing State Journal Special Report." *The Lansing Journal.* 2013: n. pag. LSJ.com. 2 July 2014.

Spears, Tom. "Saving Grey Wolves an Ethical Dilemma; Animals Dying Out on Island." *The Leader-Post* (Regina, Saskatchewan). 15 June 2013: n. pag. Canada.com. Web. 2 July 2014.

Robbins, Jim. "Moose Die-Off Alarms Scientists." n. pag. *The New York Times.* 15 Oct. 2013: n. pag. Nytimes.com. Web. 2 July 2014.

Vucetich, John A. and Rolf Peterson. "The Population Biology of Isle Royale Wolves and Moose: An Overview." 2012. n. pag. Isleroyale.org. Web. 2 July 2014.

Vucetich John A., Michael P. Nelson and Rolf O. Peterson. "Predator and Prey, a Delicate Dance." *The New York Times.* 8 May 2013: n. pag. Nytimes.com. Web. 2 July 2014.

Index